Dedicated to Antonia,
Maximilian, Danielle, George,
my parents John and Jeanette,
all my close friends for pushing
me to write down the words, and
to everyone out there who wants
to be the best version
of themselves.

CONGRATULATIONS!

By buying this book, you just invested in the most important entrepreneurial asset you have: *yourself*. You've taken the first step toward becoming a successful entrepreneur by actually *doing something about it*.

This book is for anyone who ever thought about starting a business. It's for anyone who *feels* deep down inside that they've got *something but don't know how to harness it*. The goal of this book is to unlock that 'something' within you and *inspire* you to take action. If I can help you achieve that, you'll get rich along the way, by default.

I hate most business books. I don't have the time or the attention span to spend ages slogging through long, winding theories from an "expert" on the so-called science of entrepreneurship, because the truth is entrepreneurship isn't a science. It's a behavior choice, a commitment to doing, and the only way a book is going to help an entrepreneur is if it is short, honest, and gets to the point *fast* so readers can get right back to actually *taking action*.

I didn't have that kind of book when I was starting out, but fortunately you do and you're reading it right now!

So here is the single most important lesson in this entire book: *stop* thinking, *start* doing. That's it. Get on with it.

Do it.

The scariest four words I hear from people who talk about being an entrepreneur, or starting a business, or pursuing an idea are….'*I'll do it tomorrow*'…If you want to consider yourself an entrepreneur and you want to start your business, you can't do it tomorrow, you have to do it *today*. You have to start. Even if it's in a small way. *Start*.

Make mistakes. Learn as you go. Figure it out. Find a way. Fake it till you make it. Do whatever you need to do to get going. Remember; execution beats intelligence, it beats imagination, experience, great ideas, investment money, passion, everything…it's all about *execution*.

Think of this; you're eighty years old and you're about to open a book called '*The Story of Me*'. What kind of life story do you want to read? Think on that for a moment. I doubt anyone ever wants their life story to be 100% risk free, a quick read, or uneventful. Most things work out OK, or better, over time. Even if at the time, they look pretty bad. Not making *any* decisions is worse than making decisions. Even if you get them wrong. In the 'Story of Me', if page one, sentence one reads, '*I did nothing at all because I was scared of failure, or consequences, or self-doubt and so I never really got around to doing anything.'* That's a pretty sad read isn't it? And it doesn't have to read like that. It's up to you, *and only you.*

Every action you take, including reading this book, puts you further along the path to becoming a successful entrepreneur. I'm going to give you the 'secret' formula right away. We will figure out the details later in the book. Here it is; Actions drive progress, progress drives momentum, momentum drives motivation and motivation drives the metrics that are the fuel of your success. As entrepreneurs, it's the *progress* that drives us. It's our drug of choice. Progress; always, in all ways.

I'm simply sharing what worked for me, and there's no reason why it won't work for you if you apply the ideals and practical exercises outlined in the book. Bottom line, it's all about the choices you make to invest in yourself.

The first 25% of writing this book was fun, it was new, it was exciting. The next 25% was good and I enjoyed seeing what I'd written as it opened up new ideas for what else I could write about. At about half way thru (50%) it started to get harder as 'life' got in the way and I started getting distracted, a lack of discipline started to creep in as I kept putting off the writing and found myself saying *'I'll do it tomorrow'* for months on end. The last 25% of getting this book written and finished was *really* hard. The 'new', element had gone out of it, it needed my full attention, every day, to complete it. I had to deploy all the lessons I had learned from being an entrepreneur in order to finish the book. Just like a business, it starts off with good intentions and lots of energy. However, over time, the core values of seeing it thru and maintaining a consistent mindset and output become *essential* in order to complete the job. There's no point being the fastest 75 meter sprinter in the world, if you're all out of steam in the last 25. You have to keep going for the full 100 meters to be a success and it's no different in business.

Creating a business is like creating anything. You start with an idea, and by connecting that idea to your own personal experience it becomes a vision. As you refine that vision it becomes a finished article. For a musician it's a song, for an author a book, for a screenwriter it's a script, and for an entrepreneur *it's a business plan.* It will take time for your plan to become the reality. Put in artistic terms, it will take many 'strokes of the brush on the canvas'. It will take many important choices and decisions to achieve it. But when you get there, when you see the business plan you created actually running at an optimum level, it's *art*. It's beautiful. It's a symphony. It's all innovation from your imagination. I call it Rock n' Roll business.

But where do you start?

Over the next few chapters, we'll answer that exact question head-on. I hope it's a voyage of discovery, fun, and insight for your own entrepreneurial personality.

To be clear, this is *not a get rich quick book.* (The only people getting rich off of those books are the authors!) This book is a *Philosophy.* A philosophy for everyone to Imagine, Believe and Achieve your entrepreneurial dreams. Those three words are capitalized for a reason, you'll need to embrace all three to get where you want to go and each of them is a big commitment. It's a philosophy for everyone who feels that deep inside they have *something.* Something to give. Something to improve. Something to prove. Something to contribute.

SHOUTOUT: There are seven days in the week and *'someday'* isn't one of them.

This book unlocks that potential and provides a roadmap to realizing your vision. It will guide you on how to harness and release your massive, inner entrepreneurial energy in the most productive, impactful and progressive way. Many times, all that entrepreneurial urge requires to come alive is some channeling, some focused thinking, and most importantly some *action*. This book is about the innate human spirit to create and improve what is around us. It is about the power of doing it *now*. The good news is that, as a human being, it's in your DNA to find ways improve what's around you. To use what's around you to your advantage. To keep evolving.

To find better ways to do things. Literally. Like it or not, as humans we are wired to become *dissatisfied*. To want more. To *become* more. If you want to be a successful entrepreneur start more of your sentences with who, where, why, when and what. Be curious. There is *always* a way to do something better and that's called an opportunity!

As I said, this isn't a "get rich quick" book, this is a "get *smart* quick" book. Smart about yourself. Finding out where your strengths and weaknesses are, what to look out for along the way to success and above all; how to actually start making it happen through your actions.

The book will quickly guide you on how to harness and release your inner entrepreneurial energy in the most productive and progressive ways! How to have *big* ideas, how to bring them to life, how to get started, and how to handle success when you make it big!

As an entrepreneur, you can be many things and can apply your entrepreneurship in different ways, but one thing you cannot be is indecisive. You have to make *decisions*. Some decisions will be right and some will be wrong. That's just the way it is. During this book, my hope is that you will positively metamorphosis from the way you currently live, think, behave and observe yourself and your surroundings, into *'entrepreneurial* living'.

I'm a firm believer and preacher that one day, every one of us should wake up and feel that our real-life journey is *exceeding* our aspirations. In all senses. Financially, spiritually, emotionally, physically... that we have become the best possible version of ourselves that we can be. I truly hope this book inspires you to get going on your entrepreneurial journey and be the best version of yourself. To paraphrase Shakespeare, 'It is not in the stars to hold our destiny, but in *ourselves.*'

Bottom line, it's up to you, it's a choice and there really

Ain't Nothin To It, But To Do It.

So Why Listen To Me Anyway?

My heritage is small business.

Whilst moving along successfully on my own entrepreneur journey I have also enjoyed making numerous colleagues millionaires and multi-millionaires too. I'm good at making money through *creativity*. I'm not a banker, or a Venture Capitalist, I'm too simple for that. I consider myself, and all entrepreneurs, as an artist. We create. I'm good at the art of creating a business from a napkin idea to $100m valuation. After that, it's someone else's gig. I'm not a traditional CEO, or a Fortune 500 company guy. I'm an entrepreneur. I make something happen out of nothing. My heritage is to create, build and run a business to *make a profit.* To deliver on my plan to my stakeholders, including my staff. I take that very seriously.

My grandparents owned an electrical store in the fifties and sixties in London. My parents built up a green grocery business from nothing in the seventies to eight stores. My mother and uncle owned and grew a bar business in the eighties. It's in my blood to create, to build and to work. *Hard.* I've had both successful and failed businesses over the past twenty years. Thankfully, more successes than failures! I think I've made every mistake an entrepreneur can make along the way. Which means any success I may have, has been earned the hard way.

In this book, I hope to spare you at least some of those brutal lessons and inspire you to simply, *get on with it.* I believe passionately in 'sending down the ladder' help, advice and encouragement to entrepreneurs that are in the early stages of the journey, or even still trying to figure out what the journey is. My charity, The Lester Foundation supports numerous initiatives to educate and inspire young adults to embrace the entrepreneur in them.

Contents

1. LOVE & THE ENTREPRENEUR
2. NEVER TELL ME THE ODDS
3. THE ENTREPRENEUR'S PLEDGE
4. THE I.B.A. PHILOSOPHY. IMAGINE, BELIEVE, ACHIEVE
5. SOMETHING TO PROVE
6. GOING TO THE POLLS
7. THE FIVE FOUNDATION CHOICES
8. 101 FLAVORS
9. 'BIG IDEA' GENERATION
10. THE ART OF GETTING SH*T DONE
11. THE ENTREPRENEUR'S PLAN
12. THE ART OF POSITIVE FAILURE
13. BE CAREFUL WHAT YOU WISH FOR
14. SOURCES AND FURTHER READING

Chapter 1

Love & The Entrepreneur

There are only two forms of socially acceptable madness: being in love and being an entrepreneur.

If you have ever been in love and someone asked you to describe what it's like, how would you describe it? The dictionary describes being in love as; 'the feeling that a person's happiness is important to you, and the way you show this feeling in your behavior towards them.'

Well, yes, *technically*. However, if you've ever been in love, you know that this definition is just too simple to be a comprehensive description of what's really going on and what it takes—the commitment required to stay in love and grow your relationship. It's a partnership. It's a chosen commitment. It takes passion, discipline, sacrifice, teamwork, and ultimately *actions* to make it successful.

These are the parallels between the behavior of being in love and being an entrepreneur starting your own business. It's a love affair. It's a marriage between you and your business and if you have some good fortune along the way, you'll get more out of it than you put in.

You have to give 100% to it, you don't just want it to survive, you want it to grow and flourish. Personal emotional relationships defy logic, reason, common sense, race, religion, political views and even good health sometimes. It's an all-encompassing existence of willing vulnerability, which *no one* understands but you. Anything other than absolute commitment will weaken your chances of success. Will it work out? You don't know, you can't know, until you do it. These are the feelings and emotions we experience not only when we are in love, but also as entrepreneurs.

Bottom line, as we will see from the statistics shortly, starting a marriage and starting a business is, without question, a risky business full of hopes and dreams at the beginning, but with a long road to get there ahead. You've really got to *love it* to stay the course say the stats.

Let's have a quick look at the success stats of marriage and how they compare to the success stats of starting a business. Just like starting a business, everyone goes into a marriage believing and hoping it will be a success. However, 'hope' and 'belief' is not a *strategy*.

Let me throw some stats your way. In the United States, there is one divorce approximately every 36 seconds. That's nearly 2,400 divorces per day,

16,800 divorces per week and 876,000 divorces a year. Add all that up and you're looking at a 40% to 50% fail rate.

The average length of a marriage in the United States clocks in at just 8.2 years before it fails. If you are exactly average, you got married in 2005 and probably got divorced a few years ago. By now, you may even be married for the second time!

The UK Office for National Statistics released shows a similar pattern with the most recent figures on divorce in England & Wales highlighting that the estimated percentage of marriages ending in divorce is 42%. Around half of these divorces are expected to occur in the first 10 years, with the highest chance of divorce happening between the 4th and 8th year anniversary.

Unfortunately, people run out of hope, belief and energy. There are distractions, disappointments, stresses and unknowns that come along and break us down. The reality of what we have committed to sinks in, the hard grind of making *constant* effort. Those that can't adapt to the situation let it die or ill it. Those that can adapt find a way to make it work for a greater vision, somehow, they find a path forward. They are the ones who survive and 'make it'. Sometimes against all the odds.

To balance this out with a little positivity, many, many people do indeed 'make it' and have successful marriages and businesses. But you've got to go in with your eyes wide open.

So, the stats tell us that we don't get great odds starting a marriage and we're working on average of a 50% chance of it even making it to year five. However, that is more than *ten times* as likely as the chance of your business seeing year *five!* Sorry to say it but compared to your odds of having a successful business as an entrepreneur, your chances of starting a successful marriage are great odds!

In other words, the saying 'failure is not an option' is 100% false. In fact, it's the most *probable* option!

As the great inventor Thomas Edison said, "starting a business is 1% inspiration and 99% perspiration". Meaning that the easy bit is the idea and the hard work is the execution of the idea. Getting it done. Sticking with it.

Working as a team, not an individual. Dedicating yourself to it. Regrettably, 99% of the people that start a business all have the 1% inspiration, but don't have the stamina for the 99% perspiration part!

The statistical fact is that 99% of would-be entrepreneurs will not have the insane levels of energy, effort, hard work and sacrifice required to 'make it'. It's just a statistical fact. As the saying goes 'if it was easy, everyone would be doing it.'

So now that we're all thoroughly disillusioned about the glamour of being an entrepreneur, here's the good news! Yes, only 1% make it, but it's up to *you* to decide whether you're going to be one of them. Only you can decide if you're in the 1% or not, and here's more good news…and trust me on this, it's a *choice*.

This doesn't mean that the ones who don't make it are any less smart than the ones that do. In fact, in many cases the opposite is true! It's frequently because they are normal people that they stop the insanity of the brutal early stages of starting a business. 'Normality' doesn't often fit with the personality profiles of successful entrepreneurs. Many of the most successful entrepreneurs are unusual, sometimes misfits, dropouts, people with heavy OCD tendencies, unconventional, socially awkward, eccentrics and dreamers. And in severe cases, some exhibit all of the above traits combined! I'm not speaking about all entrepreneurs here, but maybe it helps to be a 'little bit left of center' to stay the course!

Sooner or later, the brave ones among us have to jump off the cliff with the business, the idea, the ideal, or the relationship. But before we do, the smart ones among us want to figure out how to do it with the best chance of a safe landing so we don't crash onto the jagged financial and emotional rocks below!

Like success in love, success in business can be difficult to find, develop and hold onto. Building a business is not supposed to be easy. It's *supposed* to be hard. Really hard. Nothing ever worthwhile created, or fought for, came easy. You have to work at it and remember, it's the hardest roads that creates the best drivers. As Shakespeare said in A Mid-Summer Night's Dream, 'The course of true love never did run smooth'!

Don't expect anything from the world, or from anybody in it, because nobody owes you a thing. You will largely have to get where you're going on your own. That's just fine.

SHOUTOUT: The struggle is guaranteed; the success is not.

So how do you know if you're ready to start your business, if you're one of the crazy few who have what it takes? Well, if you're still asking that question, the answer is you're not. If you need words of encouragement from your friends, your family, or even me to start your business, don't do it. Because unless it's a 'hell yes!' from you, it should stay a "hell no." So, if you're still feeling doubts, then I am giving you permission to put this book down right now and do something safer with your life…

Still here? Good, let's get down to business.

Chapter 2
Never Tell Me The Odds

In the last chapter I mentioned that the odds of marriage lasting five + years are more than ten times better than the odds that your business will last that long, but that actually *understates* how tough starting a business really is. Look at these stats.

The United States has over 29 million registered businesses. 27.9m of them are defined as 'Small businesses'. The US GDP is almost $17 trillion. The small business community contributes approximately $8.5 trillion of that, so roughly *half* of the total is led by entrepreneurs!

Similarly, in 2017, 382,000 people started a new business in the UK alone. There were a total of 5.7m registered businesses in the UK at the end of 2017, that's 2.2m *more* than there were in 2000.

To give that some context, 5.4m of those 5.7m businesses are defined by the UK government as 'micro' businesses. These are small businesses that have *less* than 9 people working at them. That's 96% of *all* the businesses in the *entire* UK were Small Businesses. All led by entrepreneurs of one style or another. The UK has a gross domestic product of almost $3 trillion. In 2015, over half (52%) of all that GDP came *directly* from small to medium businesses (SMB's).

So, who's starting all these businesses?

Well, around 67% are white males, but it's worth noting that women-owned small businesses are growing. Results from a recent American Express study show that between 1997 and 2017 female entrepreneurship grew by 114%. Also minority-owned small businesses are growing too.

A study by the Minority Business Development Agency, showed that the number of minority-owned firms in the US increased by 38% between 2007 and 2016.

So, what does all this mean? It means that entrepreneurs are *important.* However small, whatever the contribution, the individual entrepreneur isn't a 'nice to have' for an economy, it's a *must* have. Bottom line, whatever your sex, background, education or ethnicity, small businesses are a *big deal* in the global economy. The world needs *you* to start your business!!

'*Wow*', I hear you say, 'this is *amazing*, let's go, go, go everyone's starting a business!'

But *wait*!

In 2017 alone, 357,000 businesses *closed* in the UK. That's just one year. If we look at the US, 20% of small businesses fail in their first year, 30% fail in their second year, and *50%* fail before five years in business. Finally, if you manage to get past the 50% that make it to year five, 70% of those small business owners fail by their 10th year in business.

This means that of all small business started in the US in 2011, only 3% are around today. *3%*.. The rest are *closed*.

So, failure is not just an option, but the most *likely* option, why the hell would anyone want to be an entrepreneur and start a business?

There's only one reason. Because they *love* it.

This book will help you identify if you are an entrepreneur, what it takes to be one and how-to shortcut your decision making to choose to be one. And the single most important factor is that you *love* what you do. If you love it you will overcome all obstacles, all hardships, all rejections. You've got to love it right from the start, because if you don't love what you're doing, you're going to quit. It's going to get very, very tough some days. On those days, love, hope and belief in yourself and the vision, may be all you have to bank. Remember, tough times don't last, tough people *do*.

It will be hard, and not for a few days, week or months, but it will probably be years of hard work, focus and determination ahead of you before you get 'there'. You have to start the journey for all the right reasons and you've got to *love* it.

And what do you do when you're in love? You make a commitment. That's what marriage vows are, after all!

So, let's start there, with a pledge of your commitment.

Chapter 3
The Entrepreneur's Pledge

Choosing to be an entrepreneur and starting a business is not for everybody. Glamorous as it may sound and appear, it is a supremely hard road to choose. So, before we go any further, please read the below, consider it carefully and decide if you are ready to sign. If not, please put the book down, it's not for you, and you just saved yourself countless amounts of time and cash in pursuing what could probably have been just a great hobby instead of a full-time business. If the answer is no, or don't know, to any of the questions below...start a conversation, start a cult, start a fire if you want to, but, *don't start a business.*

Yes, I want to be an Entrepreneur and I understand that means;

✓ Nobody owes me anything

✓ There is no guarantee of success

✓ I will be working insane hours, for long periods of time

✓ I will get what I negotiate, not what I deserve

- ✓ I will get on a plane and fly for 13 hours around the world, take a one-hour ride in a stinking taxi, in blistering heat, for a twenty-minute meeting that could come to nothing but may come to everything
- ✓ I will constantly have to leave my comfort zone
- ✓ My focus will determine my reality
- ✓ While my friends party, I'll be working
- ✓ I'll be ridiculed for my dreams and goals
- ✓ I'm choosing vulnerability
- ✓ I'm leaving my ego at the door
- ✓ I will experience failure
- ✓ My family and friends will try and talk me out of it at some point
- ✓ I will plan for, prepare for and expect success
- ✓ When I make it, everyone will say 'I knew you'd do it!'

Signed ....

The journey of the entrepreneur can be an isolated one and you need inspiration, clarity, passion and drive from one person. *You.* For those of you that seek to make everyone happy, this job is *definitely* not for you. Let's be clear, you are not doing this to make people feel warm and fuzzy, you are doing this to succeed - how other people feel about that is their business. Entrepreneurship is about power. But not about power over others. It's about power over *yourself*. Your own life. Your own direction and capabilities.

There are various formal definitions of what an entrepreneur is and actually does. The word 'entrepreneur' originates from Old French, 'entreprendre', or roughly translated, 'something undertaken'. By the sixteenth century, the noun form, entrepreneur, was being used to refer to someone who undertakes a business venture. The English Collins dictionary defines it as: 'A person who sets up a business or businesses, taking on financial risks in the hope of profit'. The Concise Encyclopedia of Economics states: 'an entrepreneur is someone who organizes, manages, and assumes the risks of a business or enterprise. An entrepreneur is an agent of change. Entrepreneurship is the process of discovering new ways of combining resources'.

An Agent of change. That's a good phrase for us to hang onto over the course of the next couple of chapters. How can we change the world around us? How could we *improve* what we see and experience in our *own* world, the world that we personally come into contact with? If we improved something, it would *directly* affect us and others in a positive emotional or functional way.

The most universal description of entrepreneurs that I've met are "people who want to actively question and/ or improve processes, services or products that they have experienced, *directly*, themselves". They are disruptors on a personal crusade to make a difference, to find a way to do things differently and make a positive contribution to their surroundings and way of life.

Being an entrepreneur is nothing like being a hired Chief Executive Officer (CEO) of a business. They are typically very different people with very different personalities. Being an entrepreneur gives you license to engage in what I call 'Rock n Roll' business. Sometimes its seat of the pants - ready, fire, aim – make it up as you go, type stuff. Other times, it's planned in a meticulous way. But either way it's a fun, exciting and edgy way to work and build a business.

Having a business is like having a baby. Except

with a business you are the father, the mother, the brother and the sister providing all-encompassing love for your business. And you want to see it grow. You want to develop it and protect it. And at some point, you want it to go out on its own and be bigger than it could have been just by staying at home. It's a passion, it's a commitment, and it's like nothing else there is. It will take everything you've got and then ask for more and if you don't find a way to deliver, it will turn on you.

Being an entrepreneur is not always a choice, it's a calling, or maybe even, an addiction. It's about having something to prove, a reason to fight back, stand your ground and even the score. The life of an entrepreneur is one of pleasure and pain, it's a pursuit of self that can only be understood by oneself. It's a stretch of the mind, body and soul. It takes a path that is as righteous as it is rewarding. It is something deep, something personal and indefinable as is any great work of art. What drives a person to remain persistent in the face of such pain? It's certainly not money; money is the by-product. No, it is *the win* that drives you. The win over self, over "*them*", over every doubt and obstacle you face along the way. It's the 'I did it' moment. And it's the pursuit of that moment with full understanding that the moment *may never even come.* As we know, the struggle is guaranteed, the success is not.

SHOUTOUT: As an entrepreneur you create your own luck.

Perhaps the most important quality of all is that entrepreneurs need to be *curious*. They ask questions of themselves, of others and of the way things currently are. Many times, the 'B.I.G idea' comes from the *questions* you ask. The sense that something you are seeing or experiencing isn't quite right, or could be better.

As an entrepreneur, I'm always curious beyond my own perspective on things. I ask questions. *Every day.* In fact, as part of my research for this book, I ran an independent survey to find out some of the most widely held beliefs that society has about entrepreneurs. By understanding what everyone *else* believes about entrepreneurs you can reflect your *own* beliefs.

Chapter 4
The I.B.A. Philosophy
Imagine. Believe. Achieve.

It's a *Philosophy*, not a Plan.

There are over seven *billion* people on the planet. There is only *one* of you. You are unique. You are special. You are important. You are restricted only by your *own* outlook on your life, your aspirations, your beliefs, your experiences, your choices and ultimately your actions.

Your outlook on life, your capabilities, your aspirations, your beliefs and your experiences are all unique to you. They all add up to *you*. Let's take all those experiences and *harness* them. Let's take all of your experiences of successes, disappointments, anger, failures, discoveries, frustrations, and illuminations and *channel* them into your pathway to success. It's an extremely powerful energy and will drive the determination and insane work hours needed for you to be successful as an entrepreneur.

In other words, the great news is that you have *control* over who you want to be, where you want to get to, and how to start. Once you take this on-board, you're already 60% of the way there!

The I.B.A Philosophy is in some ways similar to what's called the Law of Attraction. Basically, the Law of Attraction is the ability to *attract* into our lives whatever we focus on. It really is that simple. No matter what you are looking to achieve, if you can imagine your vision and see it for yourself in your mind's eye, you can make it yours. Hundreds of years ago, the Law of Attraction is first thought to have been taught to man by Buddha, who wanted it to be known that; 'what you have become, is what you have thought'. This belief is deeply intrinsic to the 'Imagine' Phase of our I.B.A Philosophy. It is believed that regardless of age, gender, nationality or religious belief, we are all susceptible to the laws which govern the Universe. It is the Law of Attraction which uses the power of the mind to translate whatever is in our thoughts, and deliver them into reality. In basic terms, all thoughts turn into things *eventually*.

But while there is truth to the power and importance of imagination, this should not be taken to mean 'if I wish for it, or hope for it, it will be'. Sorry but it doesn't work like that! It's the *principal* that you can imagine things, situations, even people into your reality by following *all* of the I.B.A. Philosophy principles.

The Philosophy is a compass with which your entire journey to 'there' can be directed in a stable, calm, almost *predictable* environment. Your success when your reach your 'there' point may be a surprise to people around you, but it won't be to you. It will be an inevitability.

It enables you to see your completely imagined canvas of 'there', all the way down to the smallest details. It provides perspective, clarity, freedom of thought and a sense of comfort of knowing your location on your pathway to entrepreneurial success. Success is won and lost in the details, in the dirt, in the unglamorous hard moments and in facing the abyss and defining the shapes of success.

It's your entrepreneurial Manifesto. It is a declaration of your individual core values and beliefs, and how you intend to achieve your aims. It functions both as a statement of principles and as a call to action. It is an ongoing, evolving state of being, not a to do list.

Force your success into the universe. The I.B.A Philosophy releases you, enables you, empowers you and guides you to be free to harness what you have *today*, to achieve what you visualize for yourself *tomorrow*.

Let's examine this simple 'IBA' Philosophy and how you can harness it to drive your success.

IMAGINE

Remember, this is *Your* Journey. The story of your life. Whoever you are, whatever business you're in right now, bottom line, you're in the *you* business. It's all about you. What you do with your life, how you spend your time, what you talk about doing and what you actually do. So, what's your vision for yourself? What's the dream life? Where's 'there' for you?

Firstly, for the entrepreneur, you need to imagine *beyond* what you think you are capable of. You must adopt a complete disregard for your limitations, or what you think your limitations are. If you think it's impossible to be a successful, multi-millionaire entrepreneur, then your right, if you think you will never get on the cover of Forbes magazine, then your right. So now let's imagine if you *could* achieve these goals. We imagine our vision of where we want the reality to be. Nothing is impossible. You just need to be clear on the vision. Now, a vision is very different from a *Dream*. Dreams are free and carefree. They can be fantasy without having the burden of anyone ever having to actually make them a reality. A vision, on the other hand, requires *execution*. Your vision must incorporate the *reality* of your own perceived capacity to achieve it. For example, I could *dream* that I land on Mars, but I can't visualize that, because I can't see how I can make that happen (unlike Elon Musk!). It's a *dream* for me, not a vision.

I believe that a fundamental building block of success is to start by imagining what your success is. I don't mean that in a small way either; I mean it in a *big* way. In as *much detail* as you can imagine. Take time to focus your energy in the imagination of your *'there'* point. What does entrepreneurial success mean to you?

It sounds like a simple question doesn't it? But while it's an easy question to ask, most people response to it with answers that lack clarity, definition and detail. Typically, people give meandering responses using phrases like 'maybe this', and 'perhaps that'. In truth, it's a question that can be tricky to answer with *real* clarity. But that's the first exercise we need to start with here.

I'm asking you to take time to seriously think about and visualize where *'there'* is for you on your entrepreneur's journey. This is the genesis of the *manifestation* of imagery to reality. From your focus determining your actual reality. If you're new to this way of becoming successful and it feels weird, going into such detail on the exercise, just trust me on this. It's the foundation of everything. It works. Once we have this clarity on where we want to get to, everything after this is in pursuit of getting 'there'.

Wayne Gretzky the famous hockey player famously said, 'a good hockey player plays where the puck is, a great player plays where the puck is going to *be*'. It's the same in taking the leap into being an entrepreneur. Entrepreneurs make decisions based on where they want to be, *not* where they are today. You have to know where you want to go, because if you commit to the choice to get there, you eventually will. Similarly, the swimmer Michael Phelps's does some- thing before the starting horn goes off that gives him an edge. Phelps mentally rehearses for two hours a day in the pool, according to Bob Bowman, head coach of the U.S. Olympics swim team. "He smells the air, tastes the water, hears the sounds, sees the clock," Phelps also uses visualization to picture himself from the perspective of a spectator in the stands. He is visualising how winning will happen. It is already become a *memory*.

The greater the detail in your imagined vision of 'there', the closer you will come to hitting the bullseye of what you are *imagining* now. It's an important exercise and you should start with figuring out where 'there' is, before you get into the details of how to achieve it or the plan itself. I guarantee that if you *don't* know where you're going, you'll get there. Nowhere! So, think big, think clearly as I'm going to ask you to write down where 'there' is for you as your first exercise shortly. Once we have that, then we have completed step one and we know where we want to go. Your focus and commitment to get there, will determine your reality.

It's very important to be careful what you visualize. The first lesson is that we start with the 'end' in mind because this book, along with your total commitment, can get you there. So be careful what you wish for. You can see where you are today by just looking around, but the key starting point to progressing on your Entrepreneurial Journey however is to open your mind on the 'where to' path.

Let's look at an example of the power of imagining your 'there'. In 1990, the popular comedian Jim Carrey was flat broke and depressed at his lack of success in Hollywood.

He had dreams of stardom and he had worked hard but he hadn't made it. All he had was his vision of success. To help him focus (and make himself feel better) Carrey crystalized his 'there' by writing himself a check for $10 million for 'acting services rendered', posted dated it ten years and kept it in his wallet. He visualized being paid $10 million for his work in 5 years. The check was a marker in his Journey. It helped him believe the vision. Carrey knew his 'there', which allowed him to work backwards. The check remained in Carrey's wallet right up until he was actually paid $10 million for Dumb and Dumber in 1995. When his father passed away, Carrey slipped the check into the coffin.

What do these examples tell us? That the vision and goals of our success are set in the *conscious* but are achieved in the *subconscious*. Once you know where you're going, it's a lot easier to get there. It's a lot easier to figure out where *'there'* is and then work backwards with goals and plans and all the things that go with making something actually happen.

SHOUTOUT: The IMAGINE phase is the first step to manifesting imagery into reality.

However high the mountain of ambition is for your vision, there must be no doubt in your mind that you can *visualize* yourself on the top of the mountain. You can imagine that vision regardless of the challenges ahead, and most of all, you *want* that vision with all of your being because it is about to engulf you. If you can't make that visualization, keep it as a nice dream! Here's the cool thing though, when visualizing your 'there' point, you don't have to have *any idea how* you are going to achieve it at this time, that's later, so don't be restricted in your execution limitations for now.

There have been some very interesting studies conducted that measure the impact of people's brain's and how it distinguishes between a real, or an imagined, experience. When you see golfers doing practice swings you know why they do that? They are *visualizing* the completed shot. Sounds obvious, but think about it, they are programming their brain how the shot will play out before they swing.

They are determining the outcome of the event before its begun and that is exactly where we want to be as entrepreneurs.

One interesting study was performed on three groups of basketball players. The first group practiced free throws *every* day for twenty days. The second made free throws on the *first* day and the *twentieth* day, as did the third group. But members of the third group spent twenty minutes every day visualizing free throws. If they "missed," they "practiced" getting the next shot right. On the twentieth day the study measured the percentage of improvement in each group. The group that practiced daily improved twenty-four percent. The second group, unsurprisingly, improved not at all. The third group, which had physically practiced no more than the second, did twenty-three percent better. Their shot accuracy improved by 23%. Just 1% less than the group that actually *did* the practise session daily.

Bottom line, the exercises indicate that the brain has trouble distinguishing between real events and *visualized* events. You trick it, through the process of visualization to believe that something that hasn't already happened yet, *has*. Through our visualization, we communicate what to focus our mind on. It's important that we tell our minds what to focus on because the object of our focus determines our perception of reality.

There's a biological explanation behind this phenomenon and it's called the Reticular Activating System (RAS). Our RAS is a network of neurons located in your brain that function to ensure your brain doesn't deal with more information than it can handle from the world around you. It determines what sensory information you perceive from your environment and what will remain unnoticed or discarded.

Our RAS basically filters out of all the information coming to our senses from the environment, it selects what will be given attention by our conscious mind. Without our RAS, our brain would be totally overwhelmed with massive inbound amounts of real-time data around us. Our RAS notices what it believes is *important* to us. What we have programmed it to identify as important. At a basic level, it prioritizes everything that concerns our survival and safety, but at a more intentional level it looks to identify elements around us *that match the content of our minds*, for example, our beliefs, thoughts, emotions and needs. It's constantly looking for data in your environment that matches and reinforces your thoughts and beliefs.

Your RAS is like your inner entrepreneur compass to identify that 'Big Idea' business opportunity that we will discuss in a couple of Chapters. If you want your compass to work to your advantage and notice opportunities that will take you closer to your objectives, you need to program it. And the best way to program it is by visualizing your 'there' in as much detail as you can.

When we visualize an action or achievement, the same regions of the brain are stimulated as when we actually perform it and the same neural networks are created. By doing this you reduce your position of fear, uncertainty and doubt of even trying to achieve it and your confidence grows as you brain records the visualization process as a *memory*, even though you haven't done it yet. It's in this visualization of your success that the actual journey to success begins. Once you have visualized as much of the micro detail in your imagination as you can, your brain will immediately start to find ways to get you there. You have the cornerstone of what you need to become successful: a *vision*.

This vision becomes our target, which evolves into our goals, which cascades down into our weekly tasks on the march towards the vision becoming reality. In the next phase, your vision will evolve into a *process*. The pathway to get you to your vision will change. The plans and the route will change. Nature doesn't create in straight lines and nor does business. Your progress will not be linear. That's OK. Stay agile in the journey, change things, work with the environment not against it so you can ride the waves of opportunity as they present themselves. There's so much we don't know today that will happen along the way. But, the vision, what you have envisioned today as your 'there', that *won't* change, that stays the same.

I believe there are two sides to all of us; who we are today and who we want to be tomorrow.

EXERCISE 1: At the end of this Chapter, I want you to imagine a big white, blank canvas. We'll call it; 'My life in ten years'. I want you to project onto that canvas *in as much detail* as you can, what you see as your success. Maybe there's a big house, if so, how many bedrooms does it have? What color are the bedspreads? How many pillows are on each bed? How many chairs at the dining room table? Has it got a pool house? How many deck chairs are around it? What color lighting do you have in the water at night? Is there a cinema room in your house? What's the movie that's playing on it? How does the kitchen smell? Maybe there are some sports cars outside, what color are they? What music is loaded to play in them? What color is the stitching on the seats? Got some clothes on? What brand are they? Got some cash in the bank? How much? What bank are you with? Wearing jewelry? What brand? What else can you see?

You get the point. This is not a small exercise, it is *the* exercise. It is your 'there' moment into reality and this is step one. We have to start with the end vision and work backwards. It's crucial to give these simple question very serious thought and consideration. To focus your imagination in *as much detail as you can*. To allow yourself to feel like you're already there. As Albert Einstein said; *'Imagination is more valuable than knowledge.'*

The rule is; if you can visualize it, regardless of scale, you can do it. The distance between your vision and reality is simply *action*.

So, take your time and get comfortable. Enter an almost meditative state and Imagine and capture the details of your vision. Your 'there' reality. Remember, only you will set your own limitations here, you are in control of what the finished canvas can look like, so think big!

BELIEVE
Belief is the *validation* phase of the vision. It's the metamorphosis from vision to plan. Now we start to think about the *how*. How to bring the vision to life with a clear plan of action for ourselves and for others. The plan delivers a reality of achieving the vision that we, and others, can validate and believe in. What do we need? Who do we need? What is the order of events that has to happen?

Where do we start? It's the reality check on the vision. Basically, if you believe it, you can achieve it. *You* have to believe it to achieve it. If you don't, it will show, and no one else will believe in you or your vision.

Belief in anything comes from being able to clearly quantify and communicate the pathway to your vision. The more thought and consideration you put into your plan, the more not only you, but also others, will believe that your vision can be achieved.

Believe in and back yourself. Belief can deliver for you where a lack of education, a broken home, or a school of hard knocks journey so far has held you back. Belief is all powerful and can be the difference in winning or losing.

I'm always surprised how few entrepreneurs make time just to *think*. To engage in disciplined thought. Thinking, for the entrepreneur and business leader is meditational enlightenment. It brings perspective, distance, and clarity.

After all, we're human *beings*, not human *doings*. Making structured time to think is a major advantage that successful entrepreneurs learn the discipline and value of. Be still. Be clear. Just be. *Then execute relentlessly.*

SHOUTOUT: The BELIEVE Phase is the metamorphosis from Vision to Plan.

Disciplined thinking doesn't just happen; you have to consciously do it. It takes effort and concentration. Great things are born from considered, disciplined thinking. You gain perspective and clarity. You connect the 'big dots'.

These become your strategy. That trickles down to the 'little dots'; these become your *tactical action plan. We all want to see the plan!*

I speak a lot about the need of *doing* in the book, of making it happen, but it's critical that, right from the start, your energy and effort is clear on its *direction*. Without that clarity of vision, chaos will reign, as huge amounts of energy and effort are deployed without clear focus.

Through thinking about the 'how' and producing a plan, your energy and effort are positively harnessed and channeled into successfully realizing your vision. Thinking leads to a clear plan, and that plan brings confidence to achieve the vision. Which leads us to the third element of the IBA Philosophy. *Achieving.*

ACHIEVE

This is the Phase where your vision has metamorphosed into Belief via a clear plan, which now needs *active execution* to achieve it. Your vision, your plan, achieves nothing without action. Act and you shall become!

You already have the ambition to achieve. We know that, because you have already *decided* that. It's a choice, not a skill. Unused ambition deteriorates, so use it or lose it. Now, it's time to *get on with it* and execute the *Plan*.

SHOUTOUT: Ambition: Use it, or lose it.

Maybe one of the most important lessons to understand about the Achieve Phase is the need to attract, retain and inspire *other people*. My grandmother used to say; 'You can't make a million with one pair of hands'. Essentially, it means you *need other people* to realize your vision in business or any other area of life. You cannot do it on your own. As the saying goes, no man or woman is an island. If you want to feel invincible, build a team around you that gels with you and that believes in you, your vision, and your Plan to achieve it. Then you'll feel invincible and as a team you can achieve the incredible and improbable.

People are important. They are the foundation

upon which almost every business grows. There is an old saying from the American Indians; *'If you want to go fast, go alone, if you want to go far, go in a group'*. The value of other people cannot be overstated as you grow your business and execute your plan. There's no greater feeling for an entrepreneur than harnessing the output of a world class team. Where everyone understands the value of accountability and authenticity. Everyone knows their marks and everyone is in rhythm, all the time. Those teams are rare and it can take years to earn the right to be part of. Hiring people that are better than you at what they do, learning from them. It's amazing how much gets done when no one strives to take the credit.

Finding, recruiting, developing and retaining a team of dependable, committed, hard working, smart people is the hardest thing to do in business. You need to be humble and smart enough to know when to shut up and listen to other people. Smart people are not usually motivated by money for long. They are motivated by being part of *something special*, and by the chance to make a corner of your imagined canvas, their own. So be a good listener, *but* make your own decisions.

I remember being sat in an empty Italian airport, late on a Friday night. I'd been traveling for hours and hours that day by train, car, plane, the flight home delayed by 3 hours, I didn't get the deal that I had travelled there to get, I was exhausted, I was alone. Feeling totally alone. And I was.

These are the moments when you are succeeding. *You will not quit.* These are the moments when you decide if you will continue or stop, triumph or despair, win or lose, fight or run, live or die. These are the moments that count. *These are the moments when normal people quit.* These are also the little moments that the entrepreneur earns his colors, his right of passage, his place at the table, your right to your 'there' success.

It's in these hard moments that the winning is done. Progress is hard. *It's supposed to be hard.* You will need to go to places you have never been before, jump off emotional and financial ledges and hope you set the parachute up just right in order to achieve your vision.

Chapter 5
Something to Prove

My favourite entrepreneurs to meet are the ones who have a chip on their shoulder. Not in a bad way. But in a *good* way. Many entrepreneurs are driven by a subconscious, or possibly conscious, need for acceptance. It can originate from many sources, and often from a very young age.

Looking back, I can see that I suppressed emotions and feelings for many years and channeled 100% of my emotions into my businesses. I think many entrepreneurs do that. It becomes a safe place. The same need can be found in many artists. Some people call it the 'hey mom look at me' syndrome. It's the deep subconscious need for recognition, acceptance and belonging. Did you know that Steve Jobs was an orphan? That Jeff Bezos is adopted? Or that Elon Musk was badly bullied as a child. It's retaliation against being underestimated. It is a sensitive and complex topic for any artist and entrepreneur to identify and explain, but the need is insatiable. Which may explain some of the insane persistence required to succeed as an entrepreneur or creative artist in any field. *You have to need it, not want it.*

Most entrepreneurs are driven by something profound and personal inside. Some know what that profound and personal thing is and talk about it, some know what it is and don't talk about it, and some just aren't aware of it. I believe it's always there, somewhere below the surface and it's always powerful. It's the *dynamo*. Over time, the entrepreneur learns to channel that disappointment, fear, anger, confusion and resentment, into a generator that just will not quit, ever. To keep the power on when most would quit.

People spend a lifetime saying 'I just want to be happy' but the way I've observed many successful people is that they replace the pursuit of happiness, with the pursuit of *purpose*. They often seem to be happier people. They have figured out where 'there' is for them and are on their way. We are all built to move *forward*. As individuals and as a species.

Psychologically and biologically. We are not built to stand still and do nothing. Nor are you, or your business ideas. You are built to move forward, to adapt, to grow. So, do so. *Move. Forward.*

SHOUTOUT: Intention is the genesis of purpose. Purpose is the engine of progress. Progress is the fuel of fulfillment. Fulfillment is the road to happiness.

This book is about you, not me, but very briefly, let me give you some context of my Journey, and, more importantly how it applies to you.

I left school aged sixteen with very few qualifications, no idea what career I wanted to pursue and no real direction. I was made to feel pretty second rate by my teachers and I was held back twice to repeat school years. I got into trouble (I won't go into that 'rebellious' period here!), my parents split up and, bottom line, at 16, I was about as directionless as a kid could be. Life could have gone either way. I definitely didn't know where my 'there' was!

I was drifting. Without any real guidance. I remember the Careers Officer at my school asking, almost *demanding* me to choose a career from a little orange book that had a set of questions in it such as; 'Do you want to work inside or outside', 'Do you want to work alone or in a group'...there were about thirty questions, and at that time, that's how kids of sixteen were supposed to choose how to work for the next fifty years of their lives!

I couldn't put my life in a 'box' in that way. There was nothing in the careers book that I wanted to do. I thought I must be weird, or stupid, or unemployable! But rather than let that feeling defeat me, I turned it into fuel and motivation.

I walked out of school on my last day into a world where I had no clue what to be, or how to be. I was a blank canvas and before I could be successful at anything I needed to go on a voyage of discovery. I asked myself what seems like a super simple question; *"What do I like to do?"*

It's a simple question but it defines *everything*. Who you are, where your interest lies, what you're passionate about doing and talking about, maybe even influencing others about. It's a simple but important question that we will revisit in the next Chapter for *your* journey so you can start figuring out what you like to do and then we work backwards. In my case, I found two fundamental things that I liked to do that would affect the rest of my entrepreneurial life.

First, I liked playing with my Sony PlayStation, with computers and with technology in general. Secondly, I liked being around creative people and being creative myself.

Not necessarily artistically creative, but people who had a passion for creating anything, including businesses. Those were broad interests, but they contained essential DNA components of where my focus was, and that focus would ultimately determine my reality.

I had a couple of jobs that didn't work out and then I stumbled across an advert for a warehouse trainee at a computer company in London. I knew I wanted to spend more time getting into computers, as it didn't seem like *work* to me. That was clue number one! If you like what you do, it *doesn't* seem like work. You're happy to put the hours in and the extra hours too. I went to the interview and got the job.

I turned up two days later to sweep the floor of the computer company. I wore a suit to do it. People laughed. I noticed that. The boss of the company didn't laugh. I noticed that too. I swept the floor like my life depended on it. I didn't *want* to sweep the floor; my pride was taking a beating. But I knew I *had* to sweep the floor to *get where I wanted to go.* I would have worked for free, just to learn. *To invest in myself.* Sometimes you've got to leave your ego at the door and just get on with the Journey!

I used the computers when everyone went home. I spoke to the sales people to understand what they did. I hung out with the tech people to understand how they worked and thought, I did the same with the programmers, the engineers, the marketing people, the finance people, the managers. I was a sponge for 'business' and people. They all looked very important, intimidating sometimes, they all knew so much and I knew so little. Would I ever be as good as them, as successful? Damn right I would be. I *decided* I would be, even then.

I spent ten years at that computer company and went from sweeping the floor to Commercial Director. When I left the company I began starting businesses, of which some failed and some made me some good money. It was around 2004 that I had my first 'eureka moment' which went on to make many millions for me (more on that later). As a nice twist, years later I bought that building I used to sweep the floor in and put one of my companies in there. And yes, every now and then, I go and have a walk around the warehouse. Talk about a nice *"I'm there"* feeling!

So, the point is, success *happens*. If you have a chip on your shoulder about something, or an event that happened in your life, good. *Channel it*. Make it work *for you*. It happened for me and it can happen for you. It's not a dream. It's a reality that you *choose* to opt into or not. *You are good enough.*

One of my early businesses – refurbishing computers and reselling them

SHOUTOUT: Belief in yourself is free.

When you know there's something inside you that wants to explode out and create, *you just know*. Even when you don't understand it, you feel it. It's an indescribable combination of desire, need, want, drive, passion, expectation, imagination, and sense of future. You know the feeling I'm referring to here, right? *Because you feel it too*. That's why your journey has brought you to this book, this page and this sentiment. You're in safe hands!

I'm writing this book in order to help you *fast track* your entrepreneurial Journey. To blossom faster. Once we are clear where 'there' is, all you have to do is start climbing the rungs of the Ladder of Success in the right order and you're on your way!

As I've mentioned, a big part of the secret to unlocking the powerful entrepreneur inside you is understanding your strengths, passions, weaknesses, interests and, quite simply, what you like doing. We will explore this much more in the next Chapter. By understanding how you think today,

I can show you how to think like an awesome entrepreneur by the end of this book. Don't worry; it's a small, but hugely *critical* adjustment!

We close this Chapter with the go-forward assumption that you will harness all of your experiences to date and channel that energy positively to achieve your vision.

Chapter 6
Going to the Polls

Being a curious entrepreneur, I ran an online survey on Facebook and amongst my own community, which covered a wide range of personality profiles and ages. I wanted to understand how people generally view entrepreneurs and what they thought it took to be a good entrepreneur. I asked the following questions;

Do you think Entrepreneurs are born, or made?

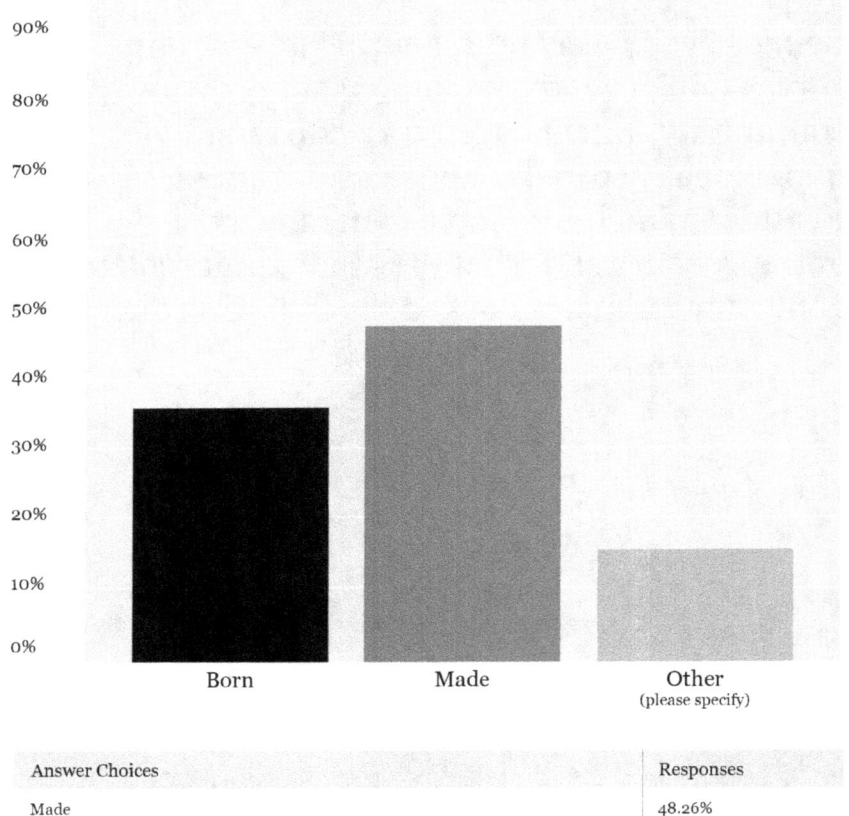

Answer Choices	Responses
Made	48.26%
Other (please specify)	15.92%

This question divided the survey with just under half of the total independent respondents believing that entrepreneurs are made. However, the other combined half believe that entrepreneurs are born, or a *combination* of born and made.

Let's review some of the responses from 'Other':

- *I think it's both - some people have the talent others are prepared to take risk, learn skills and do the work.*

- *50:50 I think environment and stimulus growing up and in early years of work can make a big difference to those that are born with the traits to be entrepreneurs.*

- *It's a special blend of guts, experience and drive... a little nature and nurture.*

- *A combination: One needs to have been intrigued by the unknown, be a risktaker, be creative to find solutions to the bigger and smaller problems, but facing the daily challenges that all these come with can be taught and developed throughout life.*

- *I believe some people are born with traits that will lend themselves well to entrepreneurship. But environment, opportunity, education and circumstance also play a factor in whether someone becomes an entrepreneur.*

- *Primarily born, but are also shaped by experience and opportunity.*

The survey suggests many believe that entrepreneurs are a product of their circumstances and experiences, which combine with natural human traits to form lifelong habits. Basically, that it's a bit of both, which matches my own experience. You can be *born* with the raw materials and you can *learn* how to apply them.

What life events have defined you? What trigger points have changed your direction in life, your drive, ambitions, and your outlook to want to become an entrepreneur?

Whatever your trigger point, you are harnessing that energy for positive effect, channeling the universal strength required to succeed. You're converting negative experiences, into positive energy output.

SHOUTOUT: Trigger points are potentially negative energy life moments, converted into positive, unmatchable entrepenurial energy.

Evaluate yourself. Were you born how you are now, or has living your life molded you?

That's good news as it means that to a large degree, being a successful entrepreneur is a *choice*, not a God-given birthright. *Anyone and everyone* can choose to be an entrepreneur if they want to.

Do you think that your sex (Male/Female) affects your chances of entrepreneurial success?

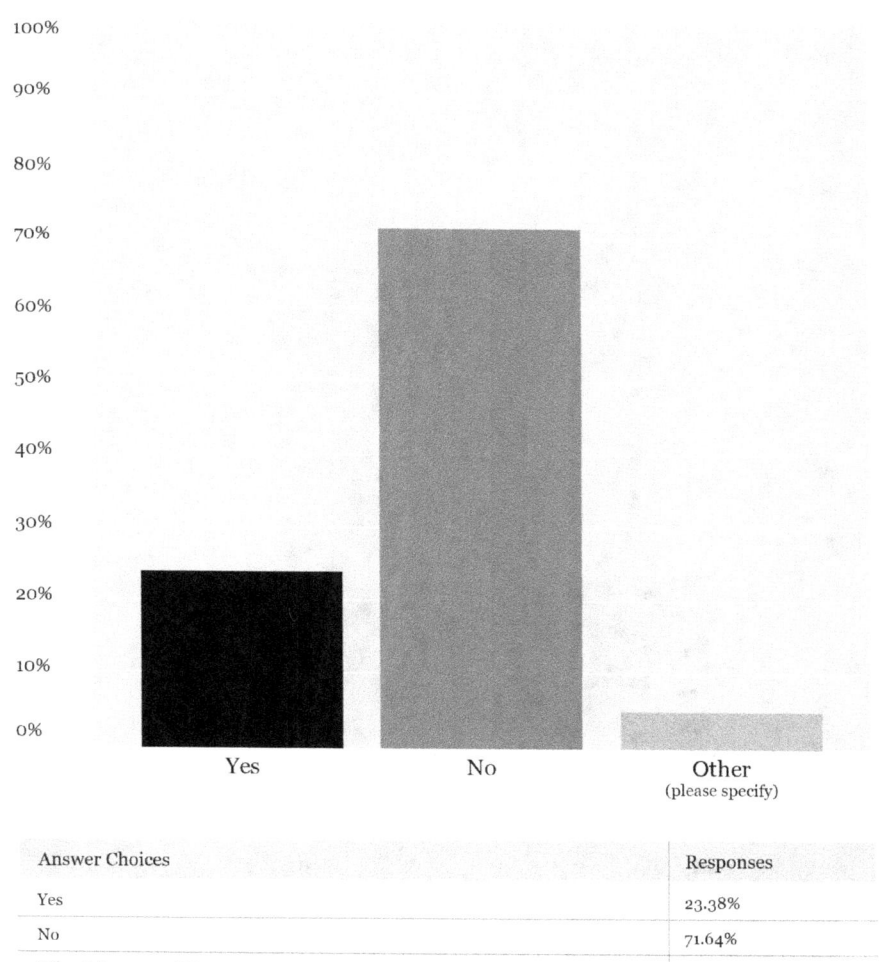

Answer Choices	Responses
Yes	23.38%
No	71.64%
Other (please specify)	4.98%

I have to agree with the survey findings here. My personal view and the data are clear. Whether you're male or female has zero impact on your chances of success as an entrepreneur.

Do you think your race/religion affects your chances of Entrepreneurial success?

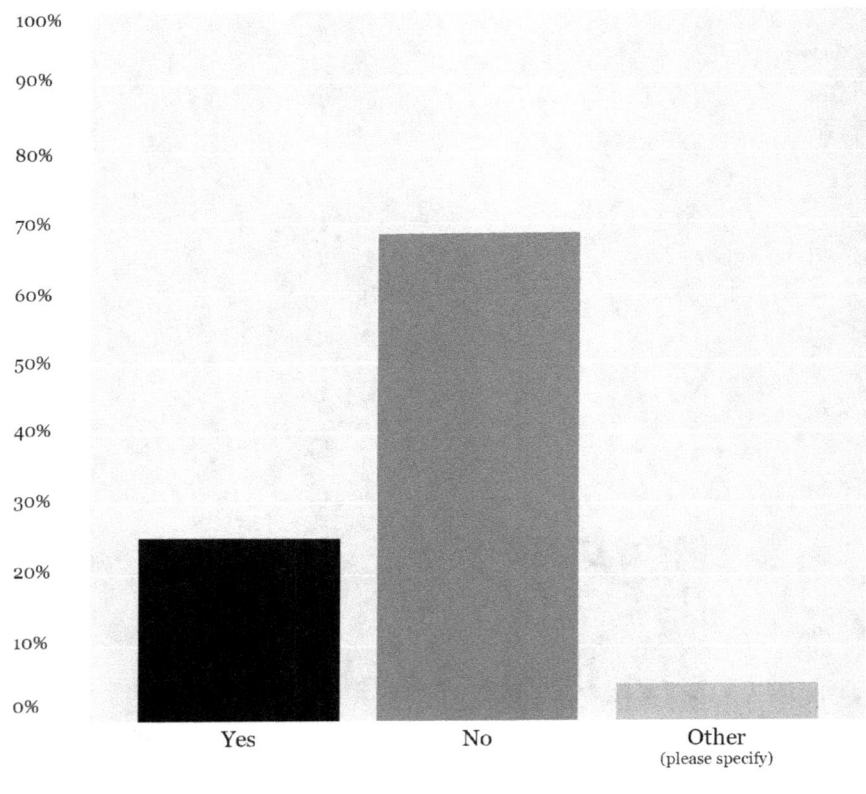

Answer Choices	Responses
Yes	26.00%
No	69.00%
Other (please specify)	5.00%

Same again, the reality tells us unequivocally that race or religion makes zero difference to your chances of being an entrepreneurial success.

Overall, the survey confirms my belief that being an entrepreneur is the greatest *leveller*. Your success genuinely doesn't depend on whether you're male, female, black, white, from a rich background, from poor background, a perfect student, or last in class. Believe me, no one cares about your story to date, or your disadvantages, or your hard times, or your woes. As the renowned Business author, Stephen R. Covey stated; *'I am not a product of my circumstances. I am a product of my decisions'*.

Do you believe that people over 50 years old can be successful, first time round, Entrepreneurs?

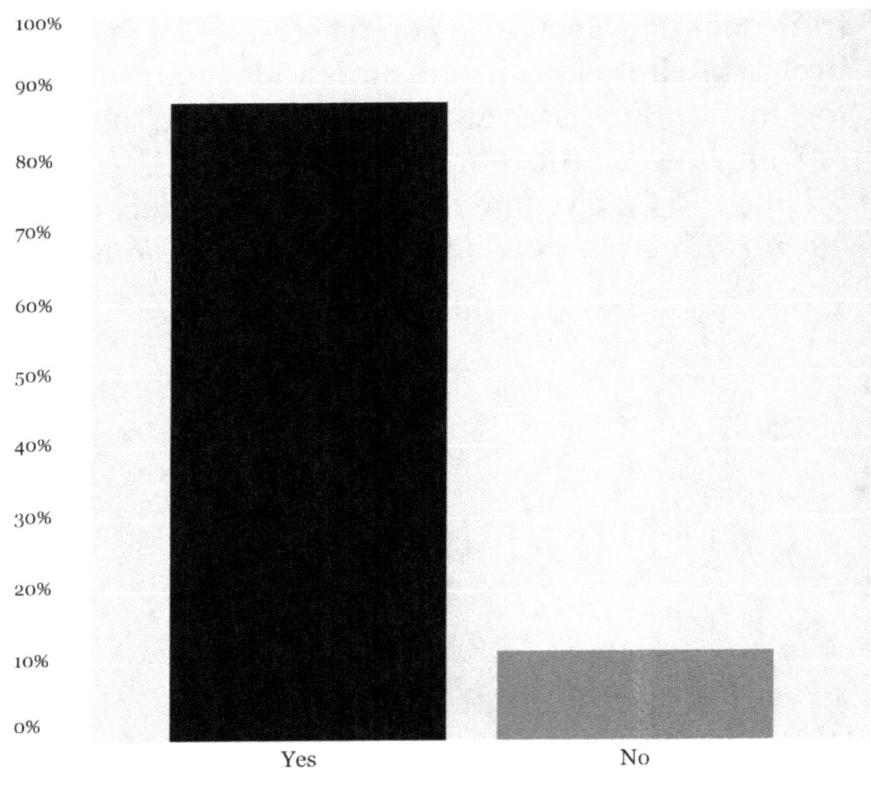

Answer Choices	Responses
Yes	88.50%
No	11.50%

If you think you're too old to be an entrepreneur, think of these people and their story. Ray Kroc (founder of McDonald's) was 52 when he opened his first franchise.

Harland Sanders was 65 when he sold his first KFC franchise. Sam Walton opened his first Walmart at 44 and one Henry Ford was 45 when he created the Model T car. Get the point? Age is nothing more than an excuse to yourself to choose not to pursue your passion.

A study by the Business Dynamics Statistics from the Census Bureau found that 51 percent of owners of small businesses are 50-88 years old, 33 percent are 35-49 and only 16 percent are 35 years old and under. We often hear about millennials starting technology businesses, but the reality is that the right time to start your business is *anytime* you like. This is especially true because entrepreneurship is not something you'll learn in school, as the next survey question demonstrates.

Do you think that the current schooling/ education system is helpful to develop young entrepreneurs?

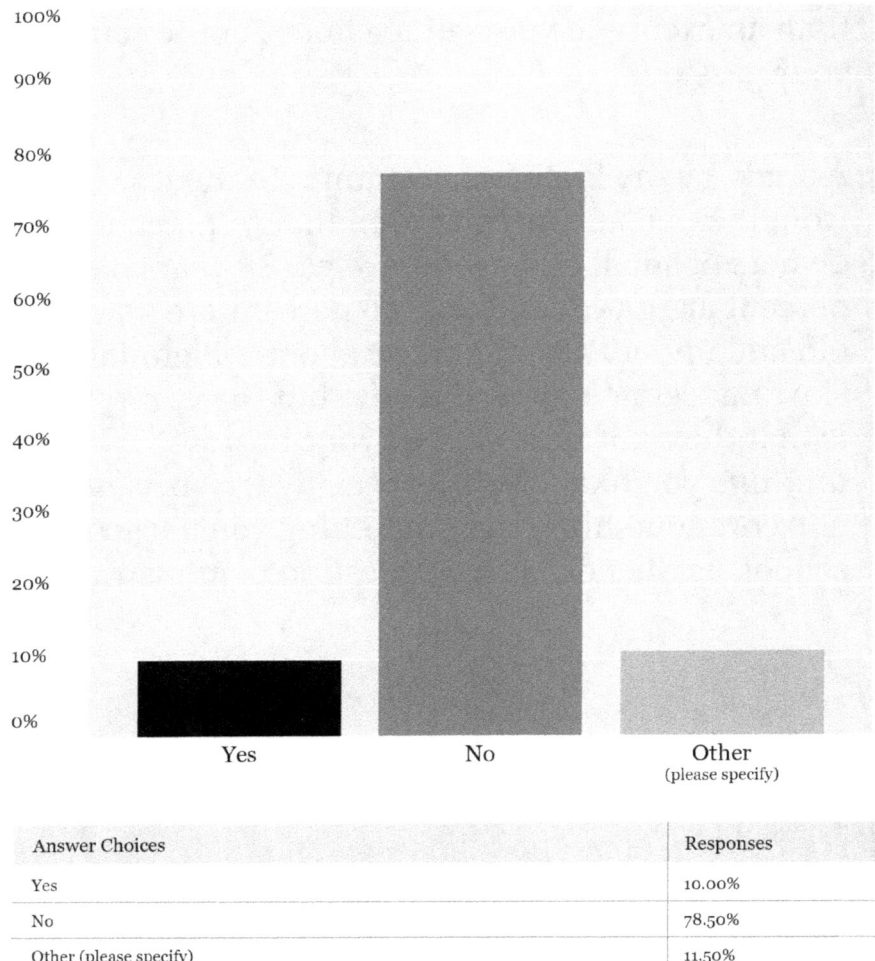

Answer Choices	Responses
Yes	10.00%
No	78.50%
Other (please specify)	11.50%

The survey sends a clear signal that people don't believe that schools (or rather, standard education), prepare young adults for entrepreneurialism. In my opinion, schools prepare kids to be *worker bees*. In fact, on a recent visit to a local school I discovered that the process is largely unchanged from when I was at school 35 years ago.

There will always be a higher demand for followers than leaders, but shouldn't there at least be recognition that being an entrepreneur is a real job? Shouldn't our education system at least make young adults aware that it's an option and what it is? The skills for being an entrepreneur can be applied to almost *any* career choice and to living a good life in general. I vote to add 'Entrepreneurial Studies' to the formal school curriculum. Who's with me!?

Fortunately, Charities including Founders for Schools and Young Enterprise are doing a great job of changing the status quo on this and educating the kids in school about the opportunity of entrepreneurialism.

So, if age, race and religion don't matter and education doesn't help, what traits *do* matter?

Please rank: 'nice to have' or essential' traits/abilities you think you need to be a successful entrepreneur.

Answer Choices	Not essential	Nice to have	Essential
Be Lucky	8.46%	68.66%	22.89%
Work hard	**1.49%**	**8.96%**	**89.55%**
Discipline	2.49%	19.90%	77.61%
Focus	1.49%	10.45%	88.06%
Charisma	4.98%	60.20%	34.83%
Obsession	17.41%	35.82%	46.77%
High Energy	4.48%	30.85%	64.68%
Imagination	2.49%	29.85%	67.66%
Intelligence	7.46%	54.73%	37.81%
Persistance	1.49%	9.45%	89.05%
Enthusiasm	1.49%	16.41%	82.09%
Social Skills	8.46%	57.21%	34.33%
Anticipation	18.91%	51.74%	29.35%
Passion	3.48%	16.92%	79.60%
Inspiration	5.47%	38.81%	55.72%
Salesmanship	5.97%	48.76%	45.27%
Organisational Skills	12.44%	59.70%	27.86%
Ability to Dream Big	8.96%	33.33%	57.71%
Curiosity	8.96%	33.33%	57.71%

There it is. Top of the list. Above sales skills, passion, intelligence, social skills, luck, even persistence. Hard. Work. Number 1. I couldn't agree more. Hard work, *works*. There is very little you will be able to control in your entrepreneurial world but effort, working hard, is 100% with you and you can choose to outwork *everyone.*

A couple of other interesting feedback points from the 'Other' section of this question were:

Stamina and a thick skin. Both are valuable to the entrepreneur. It's not just about hard work, it's about hard work over a *sustained* period of time, consistently persistent.

In addition, for every 'yes' you get, you'll get 20 'nos', so get used to it and get over it, it's never personal, so find out why it's a 'no', finetune and go again for a 'yes'.

SHOUTOUT: Hard work, works.

In order of importance our most critical entrepreneurial behaviors are: Hard work, Persistence, Focus, Discipline and Passion. Here's the really good news, these are not skills, they are *choices*. I call them the "Five Foundation Choices" and we'll talk about them in detail in the next chapter. *This is the secret sauce.* Easy words to say, but if you can commit to these solid foundation choices of behavior, you are already half way to being an *awesome entrepreneur*!

Chapter 7
The Five Foundation Choices

In business, as in life, there is very little that you can actually control. Fortunately, these Five Foundation choices are yours to control and control is a *luxury* in business.

Choose 'yes' to them to continue on your entrepreneur journey or choose 'no' and your journey won't get far. The choices are clear and entirely in your hands.

Now we are liberated because we understand that every one of us can *choose* to be a successful entrepreneur if we want to be. It's not magic, and it isn't up to anyone else! All that counts is who you are and the choices and decisions you make now. *Today.* In your own unique and differentiated way.

The way you adopt and apply the Five Foundation Choices will blend into the fabric and DNA of the way you work, your company culture, how you inspire the team of people around you and how you beat your competition. Keep aware of its importance and influence.

Let's look at the Five Foundation Choices individually and see how they resonate to you.

1. Hard work

When you start your business, you can control almost *nothing*. Not suppliers, not the market, not your competition. So, what you can control, *you must*. You can control your own behavior and work ethic. You can control your attitude. You can control your own effort. You have to put in the hours. There are a total of 168 hours in a week and you should expect to be working in one way or another for about 112 of them. That's a 16 hour day, *every day*.

Consistently and over *extended* periods of time. There are indeed many requirements to be a successful entrepreneur. *Sleep, is not one of them.* So, leave "balance" at the door. In the early days, at least, if there's no intensity and externally perceived insanity in your work hours and work discipline, then Entrepreneurism is probably not for you. To make it you have to be insanely focused and dedicated to the effort that's required to be successful. If your friends and family don't think you're crazy, you're probably not working hard enough and long enough.

Of all the things you need to become a successful entrepreneur, the number one is the willingness to choose to work hard. *Very hard.* I promise you that you don't know one successful person that hasn't had to work abnormally hard hours to make it. I guarantee it. It's more crucial to your success than your education, more important than being able to sell, more important than intelligence, luck, charisma, social skills, passion, persistence, education or any other attribute. It's the ability to work super hard, to get things done, *consistently*, that is the most common behavior amongst successful entrepreneurs with a clear vision. There is no substitute for it. There is no way round it. There are no shortcuts for it.

SHOUTOUT: Effort in, results out.

You can *choose* to get up at 6am instead of 8am and get in two hours extra work before your competitor starts, or you can choose to work till 10pm instead of 5pm, generating five more hours per day of effort and progress than your competition. If you choose to do *both* you'll be generating seven hours more effort a *day* than your competition, choosing to work seven days a week, that's forty-nine hours a week *additional* work hours. That's 2,548 more hours than your competition by the end of the calendar year. That's 106 more days of additional hard work you just *chose* to gain over your competition.

The long hours of an entrepreneur's lifestyle aren't

for everyone. It requires insane work hours and normal people will quit (because they're normal!). We will focus on this more in the next chapter and how to get your B.I.G Idea for your business.

SHOUTOUT: People say 'go the extra mile', if you do, you'll find that it's *not crowded*.

However, there is absolutely no guarantee that just because you work hard, you will succeed. That's not how it works. Every successful person worked hard, but not every hard worker is successful. If it were that easy, there would be many more successful entrepreneurs! Hard work and effort are 100% in your control and making that choice to work hard, consistently, will make the difference in your changes of entrepreneurial success.

Hard work is a *choice* not a skill.

2. Persistence
Many times, the difference between being a competitor and a *champion* is persistence. It's the quintessential choice to refuse to quit. Entrepreneurs have a history of not quitting, even in the face of apparently insurmountable odds and circumstances. In the Chapter called 'The Art of Failure' later we will talk about the *value* of failure and how it's lessons can be applied. A failed business doesn't mean you have failed as an

entrepreneur. Very few entrepreneurs hit a home run right off the first ball. But We. Keep. *Going.*

Let's face it, there is no shortage of really smart, *'unsuccessful'* people. They are not successful entrepreneurs because they don't work hard, they do, but after a while of a life of really long hours, constantly, sometimes without much short term payoff, 'normal' people give up. Because by definition, they are *normal*. It's only the 'abnormal' people don't give up. They keep going through sometimes unbearable disappointments, setbacks, and rejections. They have a spiritual calling to prove something to themselves that goes beyond the business they are creating. They are drawn like a moth to the flame. They simply can't escape the need to succeed because it means too much.

The longer you can stay committed to your 'there' vision the greater your chances of reaching it. I would guess that about half of the successful people succeeded because they were persistent. They did not give up. You simply have to take the hits and keep going for what you believe in. They say failure is not an option, but as we have already seen, failure is the most *likely* option. So, condition yourself to the disappointments, the 'no's', the let down's, the broken promises. Learn to embrace them and use them as your *fuel*. Whilst some disappointments are inevitable you will also be making some small steps towards success. Finishing a task, a new product or a new feature - look out for these milestones as those little victories all count, motivate and build towards the bigger success moments. You have to recognize and celebrate success in all of its forms to keep you, and your team, motivated.

SHOUTOUT: Recognize success in all of its forms.

Let's look at some famous names you may know that are good examples of *persistence through failure*:

- Howard Schultz, founder of Starbucks, was turned down by 217 investors before he found someone who would invest in Starbucks. That's 217 'fails'. *He kept going.*

- Henry Ford's early businesses failed and left him broke 5 times before he founded Ford Motor Company. *He kept going.*

- Walt Disney went bankrupt after failing at several businesses. He was even fired from a newspaper for lacking imagination and good ideas. *He kept going.*

- Albert Einstein was thought to be mentally handicapped before changing the face of modern physics and winning the Nobel Prize.
  He kept going.

- Thomas Edison had 1,000 attempts before inventing the light bulb. His childhood teachers also told him that he was too stupid to learn anything. *He kept going.*

- Vincent van Gogh sold only one painting in his lifetime (The Red Vineyard). Today, his works are priceless.
  He kept going.

- Michael Jordan was cut from his high school basketball team for not being good enough.
  He kept going.

- "Angry Birds" was the 52nd attempt that finally made it for Rovio.
  They kept going.

- PayPal was Max Levchin's fifth attempt at entrepreneurship that finally delivered success.
  He kept going.

- Sir James Dyson went through 5,126 failed prototypes and all of his savings over 15 years. But the 5,127th prototype worked, and the Dyson brand became the best-selling bagless vacuum brand in the United States. He is now worth an estimated $4.9 billion, according to Forbes. *He kept going.*

SHOUTOUT: Tough times don't last, tough people do.

Imagine the intensity of hard work, focus, discipline, passion and persistence these entrepreneurs had to face. *Choosing* to keep going, to stay persistent through all of these humbling and degrading experiences, one after the other, so they could come out the other side as a success. Incredible! *But a choice nonetheless.* All of them could have quit at any time. Were their friends and families worried? Did they try to talk them out of it at some point? Did they question their journey? Of course they did. They want to protect them, they love them, they don't want to see their friend or family member go through this. But, sometimes, especially in the early years, being an entrepreneur is and has to be a team of *one*.

We will talk about some of these entrepreneurs later in the Art of Failure chapter.

I worked with a sales guy once who said that after he gets his 20th 'no' from a client, he starts to seriously review alternative ways to make the sale. Giving up never even registered for him, every time he went down a path that led to a miss, he tried another and another and another, constantly refining and looking to *find a way* to get a hit.

The point is that, most of the time, entrepreneurs do not fail due to bad luck, lack of education, lack of ability or lack of connections. Most people, generally, fail in reaching their goals because of one simple reason: they chose to just give up. In Jesse Itzler's book 'Living with a Navy Seal', he describes what he calls the '40% rule'. It expalins how he hired a US Navy Seal to come and live with him for a month to teach him the lessons on mental toughness. The Navy SEAL's 40% rule is simple. When your mind is telling you that you're done, that you're exhausted, that you cannot possibly go any further, you're only actually 40% done. The 40% rule informs us that no matter how exhausted we may feel, it is always possible to draw on an untapped reserve of energy, motivation and drive that we all possess inside.

You may get 1000 rejections, but you have to keep going, adapting, and finding ways to leverage every minute advantage you can find to get to your goal. It will take everything you've got, then a little bit more to make it to 'there'.

There's a secret I learned to apply when applying high levels of persistence, constantly, over many years. Try and stay in the middle *emotionally*. Let me explain; in your journey, you will have some tremendous highs; your first sale, your first product release, your first employee, but along with that comes some pretty hard lows and no's. Don't let the highs get you *too* high, don't let the lows get you *too* low. Stay in the middle. It's good for your health. Persistence is a *choice* not a skill.

3. Focus
True focus is exceptionally hard to learn and maintain. The world gets in the way. Family gets in the way. Customers, your team, even your own behavior gets in the way. There will be 100 shiny things that do their very best to distract you from what you originally set out to do to get 'there'.

Focus does not mean no deviation from the plan; you can still *adapt* while maintaining focus on heading in the direction of 'there'. The application of focus (yours and your team's) is critical for a smooth ride. This is why the meticulous, detailed vision of 'there' is so important (and undervalued) for many early stage entrepreneurs. You have probably heard the expression 'keep your eyes on the prize' and this goes right to the point. What have you set out to achieve? Where is your 'there'? I read a while ago that 40% of motor accidents on the road were caused whilst the driver had no particular destination they were headed to.

Essentially, they were not focused on a place to go, an end point. As a result, decision-making became very narrow and reactive without consideration or focus. Keep your eyes on your prize of 'there'. You know what it looks like, you know the direction to go in. As you move along the journey its ok to adapt but it can be deadly to get distracted. *Focus is not a skill, it's a choice.*

SHOUTOUT: Focus is free.

4. Discipline
You have to do it like you *love* it. Even when you don't want to. *Especially* when you don't want to. You have to sustain your work ethic consistently, for long periods of time. Discipline is a hard taskmaster. It's forcing yourself to do what you know you need to do. Start small with discipline. Once you start developing good discipline, even in small ways, it gains traction and the benefits are obvious. Once you start on the small disciplines, they feed the big disciplines. Start *small*.

Start *now*. Remember, we are judged by what we actually do, not by what we *say* we are going to do. You have to focus your efforts on the things that are *not* working. You have to focus on the aspects of the business that you need to address, not the ones you want to. Most CEO's and entrepreneurs spend less than 10% of their total working time doing what they like to do. As an entrepreneur, your experience tells you that if you don't address the parts of the business that only you can fix, the business will inevitably stop. You can't run a successful business just doing the parts that you like doing.

Discipline leads to consistency and sometimes when you're working on your own in the early days of your business, discipline can be one of the hardest 'must haves' to master. I can't overstate how important this is to your success.

However, you master it, find a way. You have to set times to do things or you will become inefficient. It needs to be like a beat, you don't go off beat. *So, get your discipline and get your rhythm on.*

A quick note on the discipline of working from home. In the unique times in 2020 of COVID-19, more people worked from home than ever before. Many people who work from home have trouble with the mental discipline required to do just that, *work* from home, for extended periods of time. Working from home means you start work at an exact time every day, not whenever it suits you to start, it means you don't get the door to the Amazon delivery driver, you don't have daytime TV on in the background, you don't work in the bedroom, you don't take calls from friends. It means, you are completely focused on your business. That takes discipline to avoid all the distractions from home. Is there a room you can convert into a small office? Is there a room that you don't associate with fun or family? Can you convert a part of your attic? It seems insignificant but it's not. To work at home, you have to get into a work mindset, period. It's always refreshing to finish work at home and come into a *different* part of the house so the energies don't collide. If you can't get onto a space like that at home, is there a coffee shop nearby that you can work from?

Bottom line, if you're working and thinking in a clear protected structure that you create for yourself, that discipline will quickly turn into execution and that's what we want. For example, making sales calls. Start at the top and work down. Every day. That simple. Repeat, repeat, repeat. Over and over until you get to everybody. As part of your entrepreneurial journey you will need to make a lot of calls. Many of them won't get taken at first. It is what it is. This is where the discipline of persistence and self- motivation is essential. It's a routine and you do it until it's a habit and then you don't even think about it anymore because it's become a lifestyle and it's a lifestyle that will deliver your success.

Also, it's important to remember to celebrate success in all of its forms. You won't sell something every day, but you'll move the needle *closer* every day. What are those successful celebration points? Did you get a meeting? Success! Did you negotiate a better rate with your supplier? Success! Did you get a great online review? Success! Remember to take a small moment to have the discipline to celebrate the little moments.

You also need to apply discipline in looking after yourself physically. Being an entrepreneur can be extremely stressful and intense sometimes. You have to learn how to take the pressure. You have to make time to look after yourself. I'm not really a gym person, but, like most of us, I can walk, so make a point to take one hour out, every day, to grab some lunch and take a walk. Not only will it clear your mind, it will renew your body for the afternoon session. This is an easy one *not* to do, as exercise gets in the way of the day, however, trust me, if you don't have the discipline to take at least a walk a day, that sedentary you, over the course of years, will catch up with your body and it will be a big regret of your future self. *Move.*

These disciplines, maintained consistently, will lead you to positive results. Success in business is no different than success in many other things that we do. For example, if we want to have a successfully toned body, we need to go to the gym. We don't just go once and work out like a mad person for twelve hours straight and then see a successful difference. We need to keep going, all the time, in a disciplined routine. The success of your business will happen in small increments, over time, with consistent effort.

SHOUTOUT: Discipline drives rhythm, drives momentum, drives motivation, drives metrics.

5. Passion

Your start up business is your labor of love. You'll need to be passionate about your start up to keep persevering. Your passion will also be infectious to others that you will need along your journey. Passion and perseverance are linked. It's going to get so hard at times, that unless you're passionate about what you're doing, you will quit. You will need superhuman perseverance at times, and that perseverance comes from the *passion* for what you are doing and why you are doing it.

Passion is a most potent of behaviors. Un-channeled it can take you along the wrong path, but if channeled appropriately it's an *unbeatable* advantage over the competition, no matter the odds. Passion is saying to the world, 'I believe in this and I'm putting myself 100% out there for it'. When that happens, people get interested and it motivates and inspires them to help you achieve your journey, as it's *their* journey too. You become the catalyst for everyone's success. Your job is to inspire the people around you to become successful and enjoy their part of the journey! This is especially essential at the early stages of your business, because it's pretty much going to be the only collateral you can offer your new team. One side benefit to being passionate about your vision is that it installs a confidence in the team around you that they are in safe hands and that the vision is *going* to happen. It creates a sense of purpose and direction and then everyone gets excited to execute and that's the value.

There's one interesting observation I have about the Five Foundation choices. Once you make them and display them, they are *contagious* to your team, and together you *all* become a powerhouse of progress. By adopting these Foundational choices, a wonderful thing happens along the way, it forms the culture of your business and its values.

Edison said, creating anything new is 1% inspiration, 99% perspiration. The Five Foundations choices are all about the 99%. It's not about the big idea eureka moment in isolation. That's the 1% inspiration. Generating the BIG Idea for your business is actually the easiest part, as we will see in the next Chapter. It's the Five Foundations that turns the idea into a *reality*, the dreaming into *doing*, the procrastination into *progress* and there *ain't nothin to it, but to do it.*

SHOUTOUT: Success is infectious! Passion is infectious! Effort is infectious!

Grade yourself against the Five Foundation Choices to becoming a successful entrepreneur. How wide is the gap between what you're saying, and what you're choosing to do about your journey to 'there'? Is it a nice dream, but not a reality? Reflect on the Five Foundation Choices. Do you recognize yourself and your choices? Honestly, how far apart is what you're *saying* from what you're *doing* to become an entrepreneur and get where you want to be?

What's the 'Say-do' Gap?

Every successful entrepreneur makes the Five Foundation Choices. But that doesn't mean every entrepreneur does it in the same way. As we will talk about in the next Chapter, there are a wide range of skills and traits that entrepreneurs can bring to the table, and every entrepreneur will have different strengths and weaknesses.

Chapter 8

101 Flavors

As we have learnt, successful entrepreneurs *get on with it*. They understand the value of *now*. Of execution. Taking action is the *single* most important element of your success. If you don't get on with it, you'll only ever think or dream about it. It's the whole philosophy of 'Aint Nothing To It, But To Do It'.

"The way to get started is to quit talking and begin doing."
Walt Disney

Whilst there is a general profile that appears to lend itself to entrepreneurs, we come in all shapes, sizes backgrounds and personality 'flavors'. All of us are better at somethings more than others and this defines the more agile profile of an entrepreneur. For example, some entrepreneurs' personalities are *technically* flavored, like Bill Gates, co- founder of Microsoft. Although Mr Gates can sell, I'm pretty sure he wouldn't put 'sales' at the top of his list of core skills or passions. He identified what he was really good at, writing computer code, and hired someone far better than him to do the selling, Steve Ballmer.

Some are innovative *marketing* flavored entrepreneurs, like Steve Jobs, Founder of Apple, arguably the 20th century's greatest marketeer, who's vision created not just improvements on existing products such as computers, but also brought completely new products to the market, like the iPad. Some are relentless *inventors* like Sir James Dyson, who's inventing skills led to one of the greatest improvements on an *existing* product, the vacuum cleaner. Then you have the others who are simply amazing *salespeople and hustlers* such as; Sir Richard Branson, Mark Cuban, Michael Dell, Elon Musk or dare I say, Donald Trump! They have a clear vision of where they want to get to, what they want, who they need and they *sell it to the world like their lives depend on it.*

A word on being able to 'sell'. To sell in the traditional sense you need to have, or learn, *confidence*. Being too shy to take action will kill every dream you ever have. It's toxic and you need to find ways to conquer it, or at least, *appear* to have conquered it, to other people!

As quite a shy person, I realized early on in my entrepreneur journey that I didn't have the *luxury* of being shy. We have to get over our fears. Somehow. Anyhow. We have to compensate our weaknesses to be a success in business and in life.

Shy and introverted people can make great entrepreneurs because they listen more than they talk. When you have something to say, you speak and you speak at a level of confidence because you have *intently listened* first. Your shyness can't be an excuse not to talk - you can't *just* do the listening part - but you *can* use listening to build your confidence for when you do speak. Get your swagger on, be you and say what you believe in a way that others can understand and buy into.

Fundamentally, that is what sales is about, understanding people, their needs and how to meet their needs. When you think of selling, don't just think of speaking to your customer either. If you're convincing someone on your point of view, whether it's a member of staff on a particular way to approach an issue, or an investor, or any stakeholder, *you're selling*.

So even if you identify what you're not good at and sales is on this list you still need to be good enough to sell your vision to a strong sales person to come in and do you selling for you!

SHOUTOUT: Never hire a salesperson who negotiates hard on their base pay over their commission.

The point is to be an effective entrepreneur you need to develop a basic *chameleon* set of skills and abilities and be very clear on what your good at and what you're not good at. You want to spend your time developing what your *already good at* and bring in other people to fill your skills gap. I call this your *circle of competence* and you stay within it. You aren't and can't be good at everything.

EXERCISE 2:

As we have said, you won't make it alone. You need a team. Working out who you need is very important to your success, so let's establish that right now.

Good at	Not so Good
Selling	Math
Marketing	Hiring/Managing people
PR	Organisation

OK, so for this example above, I want you to focus 80% of your time, energy and attention on how you package up, price, advertise and market your business. I don't want you to even try to get better at math, management or organization. And the good news is, you don't have to. We can now clearly see the weak spots. We need two additional people as soon as we can. We need a part time *Accountant* to manage all the invoices, banking, credit control, payments and salaries. We need an *Operations Manager* who can organize and manage your staff all the delivery aspects of what you sell such as customer relations, logistics and suppliers. You will note I said 80% focus on your strong points to drive the business forward. This is because the other 20% of the time you have to connect, understand and learn from your other staff. You can *delegate* but under no circumstances must you *abdicate* these responsibilities. This is your business. You do not have to do everything, but you do have to make the effort to *understand* everything. The exercise above can be a countless number of variables, but whichever it is, you will quickly see what your weak spots are, which will lead you to the critical people you need around you as your business takes off.

This advantage of passing off your weaker skills to other people you can hire is where individuals who are aspiring entrepreneurs have a huge advantage over people that want to be successful in sports. In sports, you have to self-develop *all the skills* required to be successful as a fully rounded individual, or team player. You have to work on all your weaknesses, left foot, right foot, stamina, right hand shot, left hand shot. Not so with being an entrepreneur. As an entrepreneur, you can pay other people to cover your weaknesses, focus on what you're good at, figure out what your bad at and hire it in.

SHOUTOUT: Focus on getting better at what you're already good at and hire the rest.

To be honest, the one job that I find many early stage entrepreneurs either don't want to do, or don't understand, is the financial management.

Unless you feel that this is in your 'Good at' column, please follow my lead on this and hire a part time accountant *early*. Even if you think you don't really need one, *just do it*. This way, you can focus on driving the business forward, while your accountant is making sure all the things to do with money, tax, salaries, cash-flow, customer invoices, which are all mission critical to growing a strong business, are being managed.

Finally, remember this, *starting* a business is a different process from *running* a business, which is different from *growing* your business. You may not be the right person for the job for *all three* stages. Get your timing right and figure out what you're not good at as you move along your entrepreneurial journey and get people in to cover your weak spots.

Chapter 9
Big Idea Generation

WARNING: Once you read on you may never think the same way again!

Many of the world's most valuable companies had humble beginnings as startups. In the olden days it was extremely difficult to create a large and successful business without a tremendous amount of financial capital to open a factory or buy a fleet of trading vessels, for instance. But today, thanks in large part to the internet, groundbreaking innovations can occur in a basement, a garage, or a college dorm.

Much has been written about how to come up with new ideas for great businesses. Some 'get rich quick gurus' state that you must sit and 'think of 10 *original* ideas every day'. Well, I don't buy that at all! You can't wake up one day and say, 'I'll take an idea I've got and be an entrepreneur'. It has to be the *right* idea, at the right time and most importantly, the right idea for *you*. The idea that you would walk through fire to see come alive. Unless it's a *'hell yes'* for your business idea, the universe is sending you a signal that it's a *'no don't do it'*. It won't work. Trust me, when you know, *you know*.

In my view, the most effective way to come up with your entrepreneurial business ideas is *not* to start thinking of something *original*. It's almost impossible. It gets depressing very quickly! Now, that's not to say that you *couldn't* think of something original, but it's much, *much* easier to look at a product, process or service that's already in existence, maybe that you are already using and *improve it.* There is a huge difference between inventing something completely original, versus applying an original improvement idea to something that already exists. It's the difference between an inventor and an entrepreneur. They are wholly different universes. If you are smart enough to find a way to solve a problem that people haven't identified yet, or create a service or product that people didn't even know that they needed, congratulations, you just started an industry!

However, these are rare occurrences, so I recommend we don't start there. Let's focus on the *path of least resistance* to your 'there'.

SHOUTOUT: Don't focus on thinking of an original idea for a new product or service. Focus on improving an *existing* product or service, in an original way.

Success of a new service or product starts with the death or failure of the existing status quo. Our first principle to absorb in attracting the BIG Idea is that *everything* can be done better, faster, cheaper, or all three. Everything can be improved. Almost everything that you come into contact within your daily life is a *remix* of an original idea that could be years or decades old. It just keeps getting improved over and over.

We've already established that you have the building blocks to make an awesome entrepreneur. You are the *vehicle* for the big ideas, so now we need the *gas*! We need the ideas!! It's difficult to come up with the big ideas right?

WRONG!

You simply have to learn how to think like an entrepreneur. To see the world around you as an entrepreneur. To stop looking and start *observing* the world you live in every day. Remember your business ideas are free, so think BIG, you can have as many as you want!

Let's do it.

How can we find your BIG business ideas? Well, the first rule of finding gold, oil, great business ideas or anything else of value, is to first think about *where* the best place is to start digging for it.

Unlike gold or oil, multimillion-dollar business ideas can come from *anywhere* across the universe, so lesson one is to put your Big Idea 'antennas' up! Let me give you an example of the importance of 'tuning in' your antenna's for big ideas. Keith Richards of the Rolling Stones rock band said that when he is writing music he tunes into the world around him and the universe and then waits, like a trap door spider, for words and melodies he hears in the world around him. Once he hears something, he grabs it lightning fast and it's captured. He is always 'on'. He is always *observing*. He is tuned in and waiting for the signal, the BIG idea. In his world as a musician, it's the next catchy riff. He is inspired. He grabs it. His antennas are up, always. Then the *refinement* process of the inspiration begins which we will get to later in the Chapter.

Sticking with music, The Beatles song, "I am the Walrus". If you believe the story, John Lennon was trying to come up with a big idea for a melody and had been thinking for days, yet … nothing. Then, at home, he heard the distant wailing of a police car siren and his antennas recognized a hypnotic melody. Lennon grabs the idea and applies the melody and rhythm of the police siren to track "Mis-ter cit-y police-man" to the rhythm and melody of the song.

Go listen to it and you'll hear it. The point is, his creative antennas were *always* up and "in tune". The creative process of discovering, capturing and bottling awesome entrepreneur ideas is *no different*. Keep your BIG idea antennas up. All the time. Dormant. But *ready*.

Stay *tuned in*. It's a condition. You're not even aware of it anymore, you're just aware of the net of opportunity as the big idea drifts past and... you grab them!

The big ideas are on their way across your universe. The floodgates are now officially open! Pay attention, they are showing you the way. Are you observing now?

SHOUTOUT: Get your Big Idea Generator Antenna's UP!

So where do you *specifically* start looking for your business ideas?

EVERYWHERE AROUND YOU!

If you miss one, don't worry there is another one coming along. For example, a bear catching the jumping salmon is not luck. It is an incredibly hard thing to do (as any fisherman will tell you). However, the bear gets himself into the right position to pounce, he knows there will be fish coming, he has to stay sharp and ready and keep his antennas up and he has to be patient. But he is *ready*. He is receiving. He is hungry for success, but it will not be *rushed*, he cannot force it. He continues to observe, he focuses, he waits and then *bamm* everything comes together, he catches the fish and gets to eat. He is a success. Was it luck? Was it art, was it inevitable? No. He *observed* his surroundings and *positioned* himself to be successful when the opportunity arose? He readied himself for success.

Here's some good news; if you get your antennas up, the big ideas will come to you. We are *surrounded* by multi- million-dollar ideas all day every day. Yes, even right now. *Everywhere*, everyday. They are not elusive, hidden secrets, you just need to know how to look, or rather to *observe*.

You need to *observe* with your *entrepreneur* eyes.

Here's some every day examples of a multi-million-dollar businesses you have been *looking* at, but probably never *observed*, pretty much every day. Look at the milk carton in your fridge, or maybe you have a loaf of bread. You probably pick it up *every* day. See all those nutritional details on the side, the barcode? How does all that get there? Who makes the packaging that your last Amazon box was delivered with? Or the box your last pizza was delivered in? What about the coffee cup you have next to you, or the T-shirt you're wearing? Where does all this stuff come from. One word. *Entrepeneurs.* Someone started a business and started making them. So, why can't that be you next? (Oh, did I mention that being a successful entrepreneur doesn't always mean you will be in a glamorous business sector, providing a super exciting world changing service or product? Sometimes the road to entrepreneurial success is about providing the boring, mundane, behind the scenes products and services that no-one else really wants to do, or even thinks about!)

I'd like to invite you to experience a new way to see the world around you. To become an active *observer* of behavior and process in the world around *you*. To learn the power of observation. As Yogi Berra said, "You can observe a lot just from watching". It's very true. An entrepreneur *observes*, they don't just *look*. We constantly process what we see. And that's the key difference between looking and observing.

It's a critical adjustment to make in your path to become an awesome entrepreneur and start finding those Big Ideas from right now.

SHOUTOUT: Entrepreneurs don't hear, they listen. They don't see, they observe.

Here is the structure of a Big Ideas Generator: Observe your surroundings, Think it through, Remix what you see in your own, original way then Release it to the market and start selling and building your business.

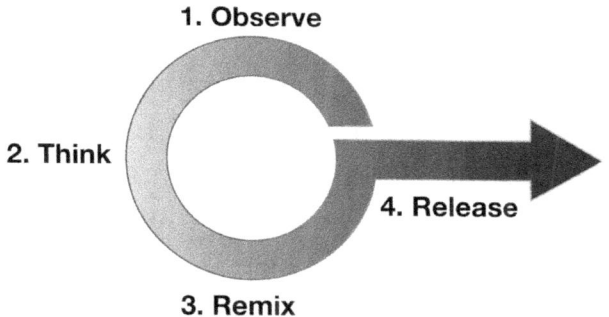

You don't have to look far to see that we always want to improve things and that desire will never end. Do you really think as you look around the room that you are in right now that the items around you will never be improved or updated? Who will think of those ideas? Why not you?

SHOUTOUT: Observe, Think, Remix, Release.

So, let's get down to it. What you have to start actively doing from this moment on is to stop looking and start *observing*. Observe *everything*. Engage in your life's activities in a new way. From this very minute onwards. I ask you to observe products, process and services that you use on a daily basis and *question*, how could they be better? How could your experience be better? Look for the gaps and *little things* you could improve in some way. How could *you* improve it? That's called *Innovation*.

Treat your *own* daily life experiences as *research* to find your big ideas. Consider it a game of 'spot the improvement'. It could be a problem to solve, you could make it faster, make it more personal, make it cheaper, make it easier, make it more fun, make it quieter, make it stronger, make it safer, make it mass market, make it exclusive, make it cleaner, make it more accessible, make it more enjoyable, or any other way of making it *better*.

You get the picture. Take something that is already there and run with it. The bigger the problem, the bigger the opportunity. If there isn't a problem, create one.

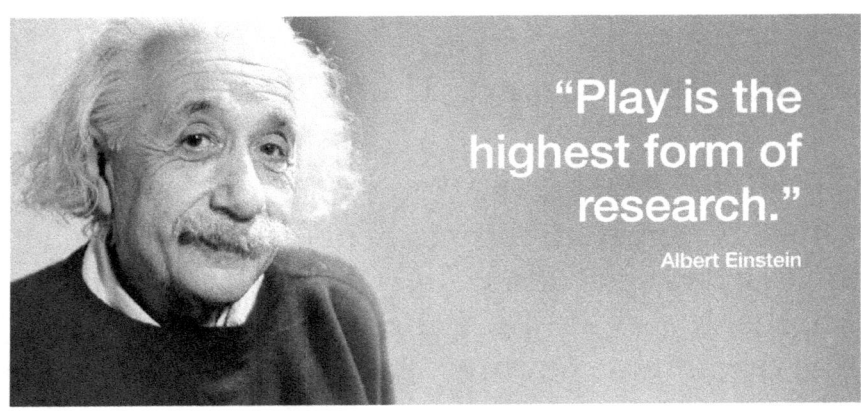

"Play is the highest form of research."

Albert Einstein

SHOUTOUT: The bigger the problem, the bigger the opportunity.

Stop looking for your big ideas and start *living* for them. They are all around your life right now. Get into the observation habit and you're a *major* step forward in your entrepreneurial thinking and *well* on your way to your BIG Idea.

EXERCISE 3: I want you to observe your own life pattern this week. That means you do what you usually do as normal, but what changes is you observe and question everything you're doing and think about the things that may annoy you or give you the feeling that it could be done in a better way, however small. Here are some examples of where I want you thinking like an entrepreneur this week:

- *How you wake up*
- *How you brush your teeth*
- *How you make your coffee in the morning*
- *How you read the news*
- *How you get to work*
- *How you pay for lunch*
- *How you feed the pet*
- *How you lock your door*
- *How you do you book to see the dentist*

- *How you secure the kids in the car*
- *How you keep fit*
- *How you put the kids to bed*
- *How you clean the car*
- *How you buy your underwear*
- *How you relax*
- *How you exercise the dog*
- *How you take out the trash*
- *How your furniture stays clean*

Hiding in every moment of your life are limitless observations that could lead to your next Big Idea, and every Big Idea after that.

Look for problems, the inconveniences and annoyances in your own world. The bigger the problem, the bigger the opportunity. I say again; *everything* is improvable. 99% of your ideas will be crazy ideas and that's absolutely what I'm asking you to get on with. If you keep coming up with a blank then your sticking too closely to the current 'rules', so break them.

The *more* ideas from your observations you generate, the faster you will get to the *awesome one* waiting for you to discover it! So how do you know a not so good idea from a BIG eureka awesome idea? When you hit THE idea, you will *know*. One clue is that you can explain your idea to anyone in thirty seconds and they will get it and smile. I call it the 'napkin' moment. It's at the stage where your idea is not researched, developed or even planned for any type of execution. It's just drawn on a napkin, or formed in your mind and it feels right. It's basic and it's beautiful.

Don't ask me to define how you will know in greater detail but believe me you will know when something is okay versus THAT'S IT! When it happens, it's a cosmic, 'You just know' moment, it's pure, there is zero doubt and there is no turning back from that moment! It's a lightning strike and you fall in love. We all know the highs and the lows are on the way from then on!!

Now let's consider the process of thinking your way to the BIG eureka idea. Thinking is one of the most generally undervalued, under-utilized processes I see in many early stage entrepreneurs and to be honest, in most people in general. It takes discipline to take and make the time to just *think*. It is not a natural state of mind for most of us., but it's incredibly valuable to think through the observation data you have collected. To brainstorm and process what you have seen and experienced and ask yourself why, how, when, and what if? Validate all the products and services you have come into contact within the next week. What feels like it could be done better? These are the paths to the BIG idea eureka moment. Your brain prods and pokes at the status quo and usually, after enough of the right thinking and the right processing of the observational data, the universal strings come together and you hear the BIG idea orchestra play and it's a beautiful moment! This is the BIG Ideas process, the discipline that leads to your BIG eureka moment enlightenment.

And it's not just about thinking in a traditional sense. Think 'stupid'. *Think crazy*. Being realistic and entrepreneurial success don't always go together! It's a doorway to freeing your mind to visualize how today's observations can be improved. It's a way to free your creative juices and *banish the shackles of traditional current thinking*. So, don't just think outside the box, think outside the dodecahedron!

SHOUTOUT: When generating ideas from your daily observations; think stupid, think crazy.

Let's look at three Big Idea observation examples where normal people were going about their normal daily lives BUT with their Entrepreneur Antennas UP!

Coffee: In 1983, while attending a housewares convention in Milan, Italy, Howard Schultz observed the coffee-bar phenomenon. Serving exotic beverages such as espresso, there were 1,500 of them in Milan alone, all of them packed with customers. Certain that coffee bars would do well in the United States, he convinced Starbucks to open one the following year. He then left the company to start Il Giornale, his own chain of coffee bars, in 1985. Two years later, he raised enough venture capital to buy out Starbucks' two founding partners and merged the firm with his own, renaming the new company Starbucks Corp. He saw the rise of socialising and coffee and *blended* (excuse the pun) the two. Nothing new here, it's a *remix*. It's repackaging.

Music: In 2001, Steve Jobs was frustrated at the disconnect between his phone, his (then) Sony Walkman portable music player and his computer. He worked hard and found a way to bring all three *together* and called it the iPhone. He blended three *existing* products, into one. He didn't invent the product per say; he wrapped it up in an original way.

That was his and Apple's Big Idea moment.

Retail: OK, so I'm no Howard Schultz or Steve Jobs, so let's bring this down a peg in global impact, without diluting the process. Around 2005, I was browsing on an online retailer website and I was looking to buy a stereo. The stereo was expensive and all the product page had on it was a tiny, blurred image of the product and the price. There was no way I could make the decision to buy it based on the information on the retailer's online product page. So, I left the website and *didn't buy it*.

Then, I went to visit the stereo brand's website to look and see if they had any information. The Brand's website was *packed* with fantastic online content for the stereo; videos, images, specification sheets, 'How to Install' Guides, what's in the box details, you name it!

Here comes one of my Big Idea eureka moments.... wouldn't it make it *easier* for us shoppers, and help retailers sell more, if all this rich, useful, online manufacturers content was available directly on the retailer's product page too? I started my company in summer of 2005 and ten years later sold it for many millions. Nothing new here, except the packaging and delivery of all the pieces of the jigsaw that were *already* in place. Through my own, personal experiences and observations, my Big Idea Generator delivered as I had my antennas up.

All of these examples are just waiting to be remixed in an improved way again and therefore all of them are potential, million-dollar business opportunities just waiting for you!

Like anything that requires creative thinking there is a process, a foundation, upon which all the creativity is built, even if the finished product, process or service *appears* to be chaotic. It's built around a process that provides structure. A heavy metal song may *seem* totally chaotic to some, with random noise from instruments being played against no structure. It isn't. It's built on a verse, chorus, instrumental foundation of some order. It's absolutely following a solid structure and the creativity is built around it.

Business ideas follow the same pattern. You can do whatever you want, but it has to follow a structure.

The Big Ideas come across the universe. They come across *your* universe. Your unique universe made up of your observations, experiences, frustrations, goals, and aspirations. They are ideas from your own personal reality. It's yours, its exclusive to you, and so is the genesis of the formation of the ideas from it. Everything you see can be improved. Let your interests, surroundings and frustrations lead the way to your Big idea!

Once you have that, there's nothing left to do but take action and turn your Big idea into reality.

Chapter 10
The Art of Getting Sh*t Done

EXECUTION, EXECUTION, EXECUTION...This is the distance between the reality of your success and just dreaming about it. The point of this chapter is to make you aware of the importance of the balance between thinking, planning and *doing*. This is the crossover period where you've completed the Observation Phase, you've got the Big Idea and you're moving into the 'Remix' or launch phase of your business.

At this stage, you can visualize *how* your product, process or service is an *improvement* from the current market offering and there Aint Nothin To It, But To Do It! It's time to get your idea off the 'Napkin' and make it *happen*! So, let's recap and get started.

1: You now know what the 'Five Foundation Choices' are in order to be a successful entrepreneur: Focus, Persistence, Hard work, Discipline and Passion. Those are behavior choices you're ready to make. **CHECK**.

2: You know how to generate big business ideas that can improve the world around you. **CHECK**

Now comes the third element. *Getting on with it.* What I refer to as "Smashing it"! Which basically means; *ferociously energetic go-forward periods of take no prisoners, full on, relentless, unmatchable, positive, controlled and focused energy* that separates you from anyone else.

Once you lock on to your big idea, you have to do your homework. You have to study *everything* about it that you can possible find out. The more you understand about the product or service, the current processes, the competition, any fails and successes in the area that have happened, the more equipped you are to start thinking about the key reasons you are going to be successful with your new approach.

Let's start with time. Many entrepreneurs are acutely aware of *time*. There's a pervasive sense of time running out, which gives you a sense of need; to progress, to discover, to create, and to be curious more actively than those who don't have the same sense of urgency. I became aware of the value of time and time management at a young age. If you don't control time, it will control you and the only guarantee we all have is that time is running out. Time, like water, can easily slip through your fingers if not controlled. But if you can bring order to time, it can be a powerful advantage. So how we *spend time* as entrepreneurs is at the heart of everything we do. It's how we work and how we set expectations for ourselves and those around us.

Here's one of the fantastic universal truths about being an entrepreneur. It doesn't matter what you're race, or religion, if you're rich or poor, if you had a great education or no education, the bottom line is all of us have twenty-four hours in a day. We all get the same. It's *how you use that twenty-four hours* that separates us and defines the outcomes of your life. If you're going to sit at home for five hours a day playing video games, then your *outcome* is probably going to be a top score in Call of Duty. If you choose to spend five hours a day reading, the *outcome* is that you're likely going to become more knowledgeable in whatever you're reading about and if you choose to hustle five hours a day, then your outcome is moving towards you being a successful entrepreneur and everything that comes with that. There's no business secret in that, it's just a set of choices that you're going to make that will affect how your life goes.

Time. You're not getting any back. You can't buy it. You can't slow it down. Be *viciously* protective of it. When you spend your time with someone, you want progress from it. When you have a meeting, you want progress from it. Once you're out of time, nothing else matters.

How we choose to use those hours can be controlled. With rigid discipline, time is your friend. Without discipline, you'll run out of time before you know it. Here's a little secret on how I have found the best way to manage time to achieve goals. It's *not* via popular 'To Do' task lists, but instead, by using my *diary*. Instead of writing a list of actions on a list, a calendar does something beautiful for your productivity. It presents *deadlines*. Self-imposed deadlines perhaps, but *deadlines* nonetheless and *deadlines get things done*. Whilst coordinated chaos may reign in most entrepreneurs' minds, we demand intricate granulator organization in our daily lives to maximize our output.

Time management is one of the most crucial skills to learn as an entrepreneur.

Circa 2006: Early days of running a business before saleforce.com!

SHOUTOUT: Deadlines get things done.

If you use an online calendar, your entries can *recur* daily, weekly, monthly and you get into a structure, a set of positive time management habits. There is no escape! It also builds discipline to get specific actions done. For example, unless I had specifically entered recurring times in my diary to write, I would never have 'found' the time to write this book. Because time is not there to be 'found'. It's there to be controlled to maximize your effort and productivity output. I'm a slave to my own calendar! I'm successful because of that small lifestyle choice. I do what my calendar says and things work out! *Try it.*

Let's consider a significant principal that separates 'Wantrepeneurs' from Entrepreneurs. In a word, it's *action*. A Wantrepenur is a phase that's become popular over the past few years as a way to describe someone who "thinks about starting a business", *but hasn't*. Someone who "will find the right idea some day!", *but hasn't*. Wantrepreneurs talk about it but never really get started. They are the *'yesterday they said tomorrow'* crew.

EXERCISE 4: Dump the 'To Do' list & get a Calendar

If you have access to a computer, open up Google and start a Google Calendar. It's very easy to set up. In your diary I want you to add three or four *recurring* 'sessions' that you will have each week, same time, same day. For example, every Monday; from 8am to 1pm 'Sales calls' from 2pm to 5pm 'Product Development'. Tuesday; 9am to 10am review of finances, 11am to 12pm Market Research'. You get the idea. This gives your week a consistent structure and discipline that orders what you're working on and keeps you from getting distracted as things come at you each week.

Like any successful person, whether it's sports, business or other, the *consistency of effort* cannot be overstated in its importance on the road to success.

SHOUTOUT: If you don't control time, it will control you.

We know that one of the Foundation Five is passion. 'Wantrepreneurs', as they are known, are still looking for their passion. Entrepreneurs understand which passions have chosen *them* and are driven by them. Wantrepreneurs are driven by what they *think* their passion should be.

There are millions of *aspiring* entrepreneurs who think they have a big idea, but never manage to put it into action.

Wantrapenurs sit around talking about it and drinking lots of coffee. Entrepreneurs *do* what they say they're going to do, and the *very* best entrepreneurs do what they are going to do and *then* say it. (Read that last line again.)

It's easy to get stuck for too long thinking through your new business goals, projects, ideas and plans. It's also a safety net to keep doing that. It's looking over the cliff edge but *not jumping*. As human's we work better, faster, more focused, more dedicated *without* a safety net. You'll be amazed what your capable of once you go for it! Screw the 'B' plan. Every second spent thinking about the 'what if I fall and fail' scenario is energy and effort *not* being spent on the A plan.

The problem is, procrastination leads to more apprehension and self-doubt if you stay there for too long teetering on the edge. You have to know when the thinking and planning time is over and it's time to jump off the cliff edge and learn to fly on the way down!

If you don't act, your failure is assured. As entrepreneurs, we execute! As the saying goes, we "feel the fear and do it anyway"!

From today, let's make sure you are starting more sentences starting with *'I've done'* compared to 'I'm going to do'.

SHOUTOUT: Done is better than perfect.

Here's a quick test. Have you got a notepad of business ideas that you've been collecting? Ask yourself how long have they been in there? Are you still peering over the cliff edge? Maybe you don't fully believe in the ideas? Maybe you think they are good, but not great business ideas.

Maybe it's just too risky. My view is if you haven't acted on a business idea within eighteen months of having it, you never will.

Does it really count for anything if you *intended* to do something, but ended up not doing it? Let's be honest, it's what you do that defines you. Not what you think, or plan to do. You're an entrepreneur, *don't over-plan and under-act*. Thinking and planning is of critical importance to your entrepreneurial success but acting and doing is even more crucial. You have to get on with it. At some point, as an Entrepreneur, you just *gotta jump*.

Jumping is not a leap of *Faith*. Jumping off the cliff at the considered moment, I consider it a leap of *Fate*. You have done your research, you have the plan, you have the passion for it. It's the right time to jump. It's not random. Your flight strategy is not based on hope, or luck, you're as ready as you *need* to be. GO!

Everyone talks about the scary vision of jumping off the cliff. Here's the secret no-one who has ever actually jumped talks about. Those rocks below are made of plastic. Make no mistake, they hurt if you hit them, but they *won't kill you*.

They just look like they will from the top of the cliff. 98% of all first-time jumpers will hit the rocks. You have to learn to fly by doing it. There's only so much you can learn from the safety of the ground playing in simulators. The secret is, if you don't learn to fly on the first jump, *you get to go again*.

For sure, you'll be hurt on impact, probably have some scar tissue, but that scar tissue will teach you more than any book or mentor on how to fly on the next jump. For true Entrepreneurs, there's always *another* jump. Every jump you make, you get better and better and better at flying. There's a reason people positively affirm; 'he's *flying* over there at XYZ startup'!

Get comfortable with the fact that you will never be fully ready, but you will be ready *enough*. You need to be able to recognize that moment and jump away from the cliff edge. While you're constantly thinking through all the possible outcomes someone else may be out there doing your idea right now!

Incidentally, thinking about doing is more tiring than *actually* doing. The constant reminder that you have something to start doesn't help your well-being, it makes you stressed and anxious. Not only is *doing* easier than *thinking about doing*, doing also gives you the ability to check something off of your to-do list, giving you a rewarding sense of progress.

SHOUTOUT: It's not what you think or plan that defines you; it's what you do.

Actually doing, instead of just thinking about

doing, requires a huge amount of focus, discipline, courage and commitment. Doing involves risk. Doing makes you vulnerable, but it's the only way for you to make progress. Vulnerability, and the ability to live with it, is an integral part of the Entrepreneur DNA. You simply have to put yourself 'out there', one hundred percent, or this is not for you. You have to take the risk to stand any chance of enjoying the reward. Control reduces stress. Stress occurs when you are in a situation that you no longer have control of. Working for yourself gives you more control than working for someone else, most of the time.

What can you do *today* to take even the smallest step towards launching your big business idea?

I see a huge error that early stage entrepreneurs make, which is waiting until they think, they have thought of *everything* and tested *everything* and the product, process or service is perfect. While they have been spending time tinkering and refining and perfecting the product, someone else put out a *good enough* product, which has taken the market by storm and they have seized the opportunity!

Their product wasn't ready, but it was *ready enough*. Some people call this approach an MVP 'Minimum Viable Product' approach. In other words, the product, process or service has the structure, it functions, but that's about it.

Imagine a house, built but with no paint on the walls, no carpet, no furnishings, it's far from finished, but you could live there right *now*. You can add the rest as you go. But you can get in *now*. That's what you need to do with your big business idea. Get on with it. Get it out there. Even if you're a little embarrassed by the quality of the first version, it doesn't matter. People and early stage customers will feed back super useful information for improvements, upgrades and ideas for you to engage with, but if you have nothing out there, you get nothing back. Get it good enough and GO! Perfection is your arch-enemy at the startup stage.

Don't pursue it. It's a mirage. It doesn't exist.

SHOUTOUT: Perfection is the enemy of progress.

Once you commit to getting started, a beautiful thing happens. The most powerful force in the Entrepreneurs universe... *Momentum*. Things start to happen, with you, around you, *for* you. The business idea starts to grow and move. It becomes an agile, living entity that attracts opportunity and progress, yearning to explode into existence. But it's 100% down to you to get it started. You are the ignition switch on your entrepreneurial journey!

In addition to getting started for yourself, your own personal commitment is something any potential investor will be looking at too. This brings us to the critical value for entrepreneurs to be *selfish*.

Being selfish on your *own* is not a problem. However, it can be a problem if you have a family, a wife or husband, a girlfriend or boyfriend, children, or friends because time with them is the sacrifice. Be aware, there is not enough time to go around to both please your business and anything outside your business. Time, energy, effort - all of these are so dedicated to your business and therefore, yourself, that there is very little left to go around.

It's not pretty and there is usually life scar tissue. Heads-up... if you think you've got this balanced, I did and I was married and divorced inside fifteen months. I thought I was ready, I thought I had found *balance*. I was completely ignorant as to how focused I was on my business at the time. It was extremely hard to come to terms with. But on an entrepreneur level, I chose to pay the price. I chose the business. I chose my 'there' vision. You fall off the bike and you get back on it as an entrepreneur and as a person. You learn and apply. You get better and you do everything you can to *not* make the same mistake again. What I should have done better and what I'll share with you here is to *involve* the people close to you. I don't mean in the details or daily running of the business, but educate them that you're going to be going thru a period where you need their support to be selfish and focused for a while. It doesn't have to be binary, there is a middle ground in there somewhere. It's tough to find but just being aware of it and looking for it is a head start. As I said, if it was easy, everyone would be doing it. Assuming you have a job today, stick with it up until the very last moment when you know you got to go. You can get a lot done preparing for 'Jump Day', whilst at your current job, getting a regular income. However, this can only be sustained for so long. Don't kid yourself you can do both forever as it won't kid anyone else. Unless you're 'all- in' at some point, it's your side-line hobby or hustle, not a serious business venture. Make the most of the transition time, then jump.

Ready?

3..

2..

1..

JUMP!

Chapter 11
The Entrepreneur's Plan

Hope, enthusiasm, and wishful thinking are all emotion based 'strategies' and therefore are your archenemies as an entrepreneur. They might make you feel good inside, but the reality is that if your strategy is based on any of these, you're in trouble. To get our Big Idea started, we need to see *The Plan*. To get things done, we need *Deadlines*. You can't move, or get anyone else's buy in, without The Plan. If you don't have a clear one written down, it's a guaranteed fail.

So, let's put one down together now.

Before we start, I'm going to make a distinction between a Formal Business Plan and an Entrepreneurial Plan. They can be different.

A formal business plan follows a universal structure including; financial forecast, details on the business and market analysis. There is no question these are highly useful documents that can assist in not only researching if your business idea is viable, but also going into the *deep* detail of how the business will look. Formal Business Plans are essential if you aim to raise more money than you can raise from yourself, your friends, family and maybe an Angel investor. (An Angel is an affluent individual who provides capital for business start-ups, usually in exchange for ownership equity.)

But as useful as they can be, these Formal Business Plans take a long time to pull together and are really no different from any other forecasting, meaning, no-one actually knows what's *really* going to happen once you start. I'm still waiting to see the first business plan that actually worked out as the plan said! It just doesn't happen. I have a different perspective on what an Entrepreneur's Plan should be. I believe it should be a 'One Pager'. The Entrepreneur's Plan is high level. It's a summary/light version of the requirements of the Formal Business Plan and is therefore easier for you to write and communicate. It's a Plan that simply assigns Five Key questions that can apply to *any* business idea that you have and allows you to get going in a *fast-track* style. Most importantly, the objective of your plan is to *inspire*. Inspire yourself, investors, potential staff, partners, suppliers, even future customers. As entrepreneurs, at the very start of our business we're often in the *inspiration* business as it's the only equity we've got!

EXERCISE 5: The One Pager Entrepreneur Business Plan.

These are the Five key Questions you need to be able to present and answer to yourself and others:

1. In 250 words or less, what is the purpose of the business? What product, process or service does it improve? How does it achieve that? How big do you think your potential market of customers could be?

2. What are the most important goals to achieve in the first 100 days of your business?

3. Who are people you need in the team in order to achieve those Top Three goals?*
   (*In case you're not sure where to start on this one, just list out three things your good at and three things you're not so good at.) Now you know the skills that you need to hire to support you with what you're *not* good at.)

4. How much cash do you need to start and run the business for the first twelve months and what will be the top three most expensive things you need to spend it on? (Most people start their business with $10,000 or less)

5. What are your projected first twelve months sales? It's best to do a worst, medium and best-case view here. How much do you think you could sell if things go badly, fairly well, or really well!

I want it all on *One page*. We need enough written down so that we *can consistently and clearly* explain to others what we want to do. That's essential. It doesn't have to be limited to only a written document either. You can add a slide-based presentation with graphics if you want or even a video (keep it under five minutes though.) Make it light and make it clear for people to understand the answers to the 'Key Five' questions. You may need to convince friends, family or an 'Angel' investor for some investment capital.

The first questions they are going to ask you are these, or similar to these. They are the right questions that you need to ask *yourself* first. It will allow you to consider, refine and get familiar with your own vision.

Before you start, I have a saying that there is 'Good Work, Bad Work and *Art* Work in business. For your business plan it needs to be Art work. You need to take your time, really *dedicate* yourself to a clear, considered and concise piece of work. Be proud of it. Make it Art.

OK, let's look at these questions in a more detail with an imaginary example to help get you started. These apply to any business.

START:

QUESTION 1:
What is the purpose of the business, what product, process or service does it improve, how does it achieve that, and how big do you think your potential market of customers could be?

(Example) The business is called 'Toothpaste to You'.

We will sell toothpaste on a repeat subscription basis from our website (toothpastedirect.com), delivered via mail to your door on a recurring basis. People don't have to remember to buy toothpaste anymore. It automatically delivers the toothpaste, on a personalized timeline cycle which the customer enters into the website when they set up their first order. According to Global Industry Analysts, Inc. (GIA) the global toothpaste industry will be worth $14b in the US alone by 2020.*

The global market for toothpaste is nicely growing, driven by a growing awareness of oral hygiene.

Rising standards of living, launch of public oral health campaigns, and aggressive advertising and marketing efforts are some of the other factors driving growth in the market. Over the years, toothpaste has emerged into the largest market sector within the Oral Care industry.

The category is undergoing significant changes with innovative products motivating people to alter their oral hygiene habits. Entry of new players and continuous launch of innovative products such as toothpastes for night time use, and toothpastes containing antioxidants and products intended for sensitive teeth, are spurring competition in the market. (193 Words)

QUESTION 2:
What are the most important goals to achieve in the first 100 days' of your business*?

*The list of actions below is in no way exhaustive, but are indicative.

1 to 30 days

- Attract investors, ideally friends, family and Angels.

- Incorporate the business.

- Set up the bank accounts.

- Meet and negotiate agreements with the toothpaste manufacturers.

- Meet and negotiate agreements with the logistics suppliers.

- Register the website name.

- Initial Website sketches and BETA site development.

- Start interviewing the people I need.

- Interview online marketing campaign Agencies.

- Try out potential competitors services.

30 to 60 days

- Interview the people I need.

- Inspire them with the plan and with clear objectives.

- Website design.

- Interview online Marketing Campaign Agencies.

60 to 100 days

- Hire the people I need.

- Hire the online Marketing Campaign Agency to represent me.

- BETA testing of the website

- Launch the MVP website and start taking orders (Minimum Viable product).

- Launch the online marketing campaign, focus on social awareness.

- Sell our first online subscription.

- Evaluate online marketing campaign effectiveness.

- If we are making money, keep hiring and investing for growth.

QUESTION 3:
Who are the people you need in order to achieve question 2?

I need three people to start with.

One; a part time Accountant to manage my

finances and suppliers, as I'm weak at that stuff.

Two; a website developer to maintain and improve my website once it's built, so people can subscribe and buy ASAP.

Three; I need an online marketing agency to launch and promote the website.

Finally, I need me, *full time*, to lead the marketing of the site, sell, organize and negotiate with the toothpaste and toothbrush manufacturers and the logistics people for the mailings and all marketing and PR for 'Toothpaste to You'.

QUESTION 4:
How much cash do you need to start and run the business for the first twelve months and what will you spend it on?

It will cost around $127,000 to run my business for a year if we generate zero profits. Just over $10,500 a month on average. The $127,000 will be spent in the first twelve months on:

- Salaries for employees $75,000

- Rent for office $12,000

- Website design $15,000

- Marketing Agency $25,000

Stock will be turned around directly from the manufacturers, so I don't need to invest in keeping stock.

QUESTION 5:
What are your projected first twelve months sales?

We expect to sell nothing in the first three months of the year as we set up the business and the website as detailed above. We will have nine trading months in our first year and expect to see sales rise from $5,000 per month, for the first three months, then increase to $20,000 per month, by month six of the first year. Overall total sales are expected to hit $135,000 in year one. Generating a pre tax profit of $8,000 in year one.

:END

Not so tough is it! You now have a clear directional Plan of action for your journey and some vital collateral that will bring your vision to life and inspire confidence from your investors and staff as you demonstrate *clarity of thinking* of your vision for your business. Critically, deadlines are also assigned over time and communicated.

Let's talk a little more about startup cash.

You're going to need some cash to get your Big Idea into the world. What are the options? Try hard to avoid loans and debt of any kind. Loans and debt are expensive ways to start your business. It's just too easy for early stage entrepreneurs to start businesses with expensive debt. Sell as much of your own stuff as you can responsibly afford to and fund yourself if at all possible. This comes down to your attitude to risk and your personal belief and commitment to the Big Idea.

Friends, families and angel investors always like to see the founders of businesses investing in their own businesses because it sends a positive message of confidence and belief from you, the founder. Even in my earliest business, I *never* took external investment. It was extremely hard to get thru some of those years. I call them my 'beans on toast' years as that's all I could afford to eat most days. I racked up debt on my credit cards, but it was cheaper than selling off part of my business on day one to an external investor. For most small to medium sized businesses, you can start small, re-invest your profits and not take on any loans or debt. The best and cheapest way to raise cash is *always* from your own sales.

Sometimes people like to make investing in startup businesses a complex process. It doesn't have to be. It's pretty simple actually. When I review a business to invest in, I stick to my '4Ps' rule. Plan, People, Passion, Price.

Firstly, let's see the *Plan*. No plan, *no* investment. It's not so much to ask for is it! Fully consider your plan and write it down. *People*; will you work well with your team and will they work well with you? There will be some brutally hard times, so you need to be able to have fun as you drive the business forward. *Passion*; do you love what you are doing? Do you believe in yourself and the business 100%? How much have you put into the business yourself to date in time, effort and finance? *Price*; is the business valued appropriately to give me as the investor maximum chance to add value, get to the crystallization 'exit; or business sale point, and make a profit from my investment today?

Whatever your business, try hard to avoid buying big expensive capital equipment at the beginning. Rent and *test* the business first. For example, say you want to start making and selling fashion items. It's a much safer option to rent a market stall for 6 months at the beginning than to commit to an expensive retail outlet. You can always trade up to the retail outlet, but it's tough to go the other way.

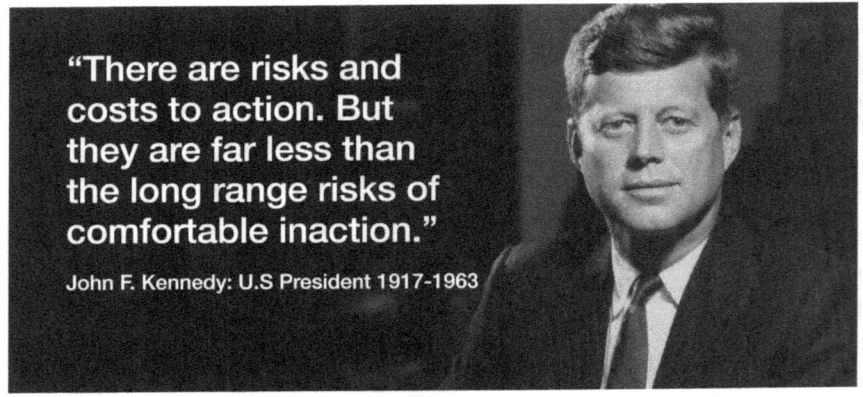

"There are risks and costs to action. But they are far less than the long range risks of comfortable inaction."
John F. Kennedy: U.S President 1917-1963

The Entrepreneurs Plan starts the process of *validation* of your Big Idea, to yourself and others, in a formal way. It gets you past just the idea and evolves it to an executional plan. All the businesses you love interacting and buying from today, started with a plan that became the *structure* of their entrepreneurial business success. I guarantee that if you can express your business idea in the format, or similar format, to the above, you will get peoples' attention. You may not get their money, but you will get the opportunity to pitch your plan in a clear, concise and confident way as an entrepreneur.

One more thing to consider, are two heads better than one when you start a business? The data shows that two founding partners have significantly better odds of driving a business to success than one. The ability to rely on each other to share the burden, consider the risks, get creative together, take on specific areas of responsibility, and to motivate each other are all absolutely critical during the early stages of growth. Having the whole business to yourself is tempting, but 100% of a grape sized business is worth less than 50% of a grapefruit sized one! This is one case where one plus one *could* be more than the sum of the parts. Do you know anyone who could be a good business partner and has a different, but complimentary set of skills, to you?

Do the exercise. Write your Plan and execute. That's how entrepreneurial success is achieved and that's the fundamental principle of the Aint't Nothin To It But To Do It Philosophy. Less Talk, More DO!

Chapter 12
The Art of positive Failure

This may just be the most important chapter in the book.

Here's the big misunderstanding most people have about failure. That it's the *opposite* of success. It's not. As in life, failure is an essential and integral process on the path to success in business. You actually learn very little from success and you learn *huge* amounts from failure. Just like pain or pleasure, neither failure nor success are constant states. They move, they shape-shift, they combine to shape the journey. So, if you're in a period of perceived failure, look around and figure out what went wrong, because understanding that is part of your on-going journey to *success*.

Now, if you're in a period of perceived success, do the *same* exercise. Why are you feeling successful? As humans, we seem to do a very good job at evaluating why we failed and not so much evaluation when we succeed.

It's important to understand the reasons for both as it all adds up to be one big merry-go round. At the time, it's impossible to connect the dots of any individual success or failure. You can only connect the dots when you look *back* on the journey, or chapters of the journey. As time marches on, you see the dots connect and the moments of failure or success reveal themselves as one story.

In the 2017, 'National Entrepreneurial Assessment for the United States of America' study by the Global Entrepreneur Monitor (GEM) it found that among people who 'perceive opportunity' to start a business, the *fear of failure* rate vacillates between 32% to 37% among 18 to 54 year olds, but the oldest group, 65 to 74 year olds, had the *lowest* fear of failure rate at just 18%. In other words, the older you get, the less worried you are about failing! Maybe its ego, maybe its awareness of time, but whatever it is, it's an interesting point that if you're over 65, help encourage your younger potential entrepreneurs to *embrace* the possibility of failure.

At nine years old, I was at a very expensive, private English school and I remember my maths teacher (Mr Gafney) making me stand up in front of the whole class and asking me to explain why I had come last in class for three consecutive terms. *'Why have you failed boy?'* he said. I recall that I just stood there and took it. Didn't say anything, didn't have an answer. Don't actually remember most of the situation at the time, *but,* I remember the *feeling* of being a failure.

At twelve years old, I failed to pass my entrance exam to my secondary school. At sixteen, I left high school with minimal qualifications having failed most of my exams. I went out blindly into the world, with no idea of who I was or what I wanted to be or do. I went to several interviews and failed to get the jobs. I remember one in particular was for a real estate sales job, that I really wanted and still didn't get. Then at eighteen I applied for a job at Ford. It was an apprenticeship and over five hundred young adults under eighteen applied. I got to the last two and was called into the General Manager's office where I remember him asking me, 'what do you want to be doing in five years' and I said, instinctively, 'your job'. He laughed, I didn't. It wasn't a joke. It was aspirational, *maybe,* but it wasn't a joke. I got the call. I got the job! Success! After six months, I quit. If that was 'work', I didn't want it. I didn't like the people and I realized I didn't want to be timed for a forty-five-minute lunch break for the next forty years. I guess I had a deep issue with 'the rules'. At nineteen years old, I failed my driving test twice. At twenty-two, I failed my motorbike license five times! By the time I was thirty-four, I had started three businesses and two of them had failed. Failure hurts. It's *supposed* to hurt. But, as one of the Founding Fathers of the United States, Benjamin Franklin said; what hurts *instructs*....in people and in businesses. Don't forget, you're more likely to succeed if you've failed than if you've *never tried*.

So, why do businesses fail?

The statistics tell us that Founders of previously successful businesses have a 30% chance of success with their next venture, founders who have failed at a prior business have a 20% chance of succeeding versus an 18% chance of success for first time entrepreneurs. You can probably guess why.

Although you learn a lot from success, failure also teaches valuable lessons about what *not* to do. If you're a first-time entrepreneur, you haven't learned those lessons and without the benefit of an experienced advisor you *will* learn them first hand and you will get the scar tissue. Like we all do.

However, failure, like pain, is not a permanent state. It subsides. A failed relationship, like a failed business, hurts. *Deeply*. At times it feels like you can't recover to be your former self and yet you can and we all do. However, we keep moving forward, we apply the lessons we learned. We get better.

If you're afraid of failing, you won't get very far. With anything. In business, in sports, in life. To be a successful entrepreneur, you have to be *creative*. It's the only commodity that you need to start a business. To be creative, you have to be ready to be *vulnerable*. To allow yourself to make mistakes. To be *naked*. Maybe my next book should be called "The Naked Entrepreneur"! You simply *have* to lay yourself bare and be ready to embrace failing as much as success in order to achieve your goals and vision.

Feeling vulnerable and the experience of humiliation is one of the worst experiences in the world. We are all scared of it. But to create a business you believe in, express an idea you believe in, to create art of any kind that you believe in, you *have* to put yourself in a place of vulnerability. You have to invite it in to have any chance of making it. The fact is that other people will be critical of what you do and how you do it. So, get used to it. The only way to avoid feeling vulnerable, or humiliated, or criticized is to not try and do anything interesting, or different, *ever*.

Below is a picture of me at one of the first events I held at one of my later companies. I was very excited as I had a stand at a show and I thought my service was very cool and interesting, I was going to make it big! You know how many people stopped by the stand over a two-day period. No one. NO-ONE! I was crushed. Total failure!

At the time, I had no idea it was putting high-octane fuel into my entrepreneur engines to prove 'them' wrong. (No idea who 'they' are by the way). I'll work even *harder*, innovate even more *dramatically*. Eight years after this picture of my 'failure' was taken, the business sold for tens of millions.

Being an early stage Entrepreneur can be a lonely place!

As basic as it sounds, the vast majority of people don't realize their dreams because they are too scared to fail, even in small ways. They don't even *ask* for help. They're scared that if they call up that company, or that purchasing manager, retailer, supplier, or investor, that the person on the other end of the phone will reject them, or laugh at them. People's fear of being laughed at, ridiculed or rejected kills more dreams than anything else. Asking for help sounds simple, but it's amazing how many early stage entrepreneurs I meet that don't get the *huge* value that can be gained by just *asking*.

Always, always, always, always, *always* ask for help. It costs you nothing to ask and you will be surprised how helpful most people can be when you simply ask for their help.

It's one of the founding elements of my success. *Just ask.* I guarantee you that most people will be delighted to help.

As an example of how powerful asking for help can be, I had a call with an early stage entrepreneur recently who is building a CRM (Customer Relationship Management) platform, she called me for some advice and right away I could see that her path of least resistance to get this off the ground and pursue a sale of her early business was to build it for Salesforce. I knew a few people at Salesforce, so I connected her and set up a call. It's not a guarantee of any success but simply by picking up the phone and asking someone that may be able to help her it has accelerated her efforts and focus and potentially found her an investor. You know what it cost her? *Nothing* except the initiative and courage to go ask for help. Try it, you will be surprised how much support you get!

I have to be honest; every time I've asked anyone for help, they've helped. Anytime anyone has asked me for help, I've helped. I think that's a natural human tendency. To help each other if we can.

An entrepreneur does not view failure as defeat or as 'The End'. Failure is not nice. It's horrible. At the time it can be almost overwhelming. But the feeling passes and the value of the experience remains. Almost like a magic 'learning residue'. The value of failure sinks into your blood, your DNA and is distilled to powerful forces that you control. Whatever it takes to heal the fail wound, converts into powerful forces in the entrepreneur's character kit. Drive, ambition, doggedness, the will to win, tenacity.

Failure happens; otherwise there's no risk. Without risk, there can be no reward. That's just the way it works. It's an essential process from which to yield *value*. We never fear failure, we don't go into the business, or any situation, expecting to fail. We go in prepared to *win, grow, and succeed*. We understand the discipline and effort that those expectations require and as entrepreneurs, we make those sacrifices.

As you get more experience in life and entrepreneurship, you come to understand that failure is an essential component of success. It's actually a part of the DNA of the overall road *to* success. So, I say, get used to it, understand how to extract value from failure, but don't welcome it.

Be smart enough to recognize that after enough time has passed and you have worked as smart and as hard as you can, if the business isn't taking off, take the lessons from it and try something new. Failure is simply the opportunity to begin again, this time 'more experienced'.

There's one simple rule to managing failure and rejection. Never, ever, *ever* take it personally. It isn't personal. Detach yourself. It's a response upon which you must work.

Rejection, failure, loss. Whatever the circumstance, this is professional. You are a professional. It's never personal, unless you make it so. Get used to getting 'no', and the world not being fair and not getting what you think you deserve. No one owes you *anything*. You think you're 'owed' because you worked hard? Think again!

Leave all that thinking at the door if you're seriously considering being an entrepreneur.

It's never personal; so, don't confuse your emotions. Your personal emotional energy is far better harnessed towards achieving your own goals. It's very important to understand it's your *principles*, not your feelings, that will lead you to success. Once your feelings have the reigns, you're out of logical control. You're using emotion instead of reason to make decisions and there are very few situations where that ends well. Sometimes, even the most balanced entrepreneurs fall prey to this, especially due to pressure. It's no different than any battle that's ever been fought, any team that has gone out to beat another, any psychological warfare that's been deployed in a boxing match or any other example. If they can get to you, get under your skin and get you making emotion-based decisions, it's pretty much already over for you. This leads us back to discipline and its importance, especially, in the rough times. It's easy to be disciplined when things are going well, its *supremely hard* to stay disciplined for yourself, for your team, when the seas are rough. It's during those hard moments that you must lead, when you must stay focused and keep your eye firmly focused on winning the *war*, not every *battle* on your way to 'there'.

SHOUTOUT: Never, ever, *ever* take rejection or failure personally.

We looked at some examples in Chapter Two of people who most of us know only as *successes*, but who endured harsh failures along the way. Remember, it's not supposed to be easy. Nothing ever worth doing, being or aspiring to is easy. It's hard. Very hard. So how does an entrepreneur process failure and convert their rejections into positive energy?

Let me paint the analogy of learning to ride a bike. You get on. You *want* to ride. You try. You fall. You bruise. You get up. You try again. You go further than last time. You fall.

You *bleed*. You get up. You ride. You go further than you thought. You're surprised you did. You get nervous. You fall. You scar. You get up. You can ride. You're riding. Someone faster passes you. You speed up. You're competing.

It's a cycle (excuse the pun). You learn from the fall and apply your education of the cause of the fall to avoid it next time. The fall delivers value. Negative experience converted into *positive* educational value.

The key to being a great entrepreneur is to have the right attitude towards failure. This is so important.

Let's start with some basic psychology with two sentences;

1. You just *failed* at something.

2. You just *learnt* something.

The first sentence perspective is only true if you decide *not to get back on the bike*. If you just got back on the bike, you just got *better*. The original event remains unchanged, ie, you fell off the bike, but the outcome is *wholly* different.

Entrepreneurs *keep getting on the bike*. It's a lifetime experience. There is no perfect ride, but there is the *pursuit* of the perfect ride and that is the addiction of the disease we call entrepreneurialism in its most acute sense. The comebacks from failures are always bigger than the setbacks.

SHOUTOUT: Failure, just as success, is never final. It's always a journey.

Vera Wang failed to make the 1968 US Olympic figure- skating team. Then she became an editor at Vogue, but was passed over for the editor-in-chief position. She began designing wedding gowns at age 40 and today is one of the premier designers in the fashion industry, with a business worth over $1 billion.

In what might be one of the most discouraging statements of all time, Thomas Edison's mother was told via a note from his school teachers that he was 'too stupid to learn anything', that the school would no longer spend time trying to educate him and that he should be home tutored by his mother.

At the time, Edison's mother did not want to discourage the young boy and instead told him the school note said he was too *smart* for the school and that they had recommended he be taught at home. Years after his mother's death, Edison found the note from the school. Edison went on to hold more than 1,000 patents, including the phonograph and practical electric lamp.

The editor of the local paper Disney worked for told him that he 'lacked imagination and had no good ideas'. Undeterred, Disney went on to create the cultural icon that bears his name. Disney's view on failure; *"I think it's important to have a good hard failure when you're young...*

Because it makes you kind of aware of what can happen to you. Because of it I've never had any fear in my whole life when we've been near collapse and all of that. I've never been afraid."

J.K Rowling was a broke, depressed, divorced single mother simultaneously writing a novel while studying. She is now one of the richest women in the world, Rowling reflects on her early failures: *"It is impossible to live without failing at something, unless you live so cautiously that you might as well not have lived at all – in which case, you fail by default.*

Michael Jordan was cut from his high school basketball team. Six Championships and five MVPs later, Jordan became arguably the greatest basketball player of all time. Jordan famously said: *"I have missed more than 9,000 shots in my career. I have lost almost 300 games. On 26 occasions I have been entrusted to take the game winning shot, and I missed. I have failed over and over and over again in my life. And that is why I succeed."*

I love these stories. A failure is only a failure when no lessons or learning comes from it. I started and failed in businesses until I got to thirty-five years old, the examples in this chapter prove that the journey is *never over* until you want it to be. You can start and *restart* as many times as you have the desire to do so. As long as you're learning as you go, you're already succeeding. So, keep getting back on your bike.

As Winston Churchill once remarked; "Success is stumbling from failure to failure with no loss of enthusiasm."

OK, enough of the 'F' word! Your basically ready. Let's move on and find out in the next Chapter what happens when you make it Big!

Chapter 13
Be Careful What You Wish For

Wow! This is amazing! I made it! Whooohhhooo!! I'm a successful entrepreneur! I'm *there*!

Wait a minute, what just happened?

There is a 'crystallization' moment when you arrive at your 'there' point. Your vision has become your reality. Its euphoric, its emotional, its real. However, for many it's also a fleeting moment of euphoria as you always *expected* to get here. Here you are. You planned for this, you constructed this, you decided this at the beginning of the journey. So, when you get to your 'there' point, you're not surprised. Your success is expected. Your success is not random. It's been planned and executed for you, by you. You are where you wanted to get to. So how do you feel?

All entrepreneurs are driven to achieve our visions if we choose to do so. Yet, most of us give almost no thought to the reality of what happens when we actually achieve it until we actually get there. From my experience, the single biggest feeling of success is the sense of achievement. It is the most impactful sense of getting 'there'. *Achievement.* It may be hard to understand when you're starting out that it's a bigger buzz than the money, or the adulation, or anything you go and buy. Your own sense of achievement is the *lasting currency* of success. If anything, that's what changes you as an individual once you make it. Your self-belief was always there that you *could* do it, the difference now is that you've *done* it. Yes, as a byproduct of getting 'there' you typically make a lot of money. However, the money, to a large degree, doesn't have either a significant impact on your character, or a lasting sense of euphoria.

If you are a nice person who is considerate of others *before* you make it big, having money won't change that. Equally, if you are an arrogant, self-centered and selfish person, having more money won't change that behavior either!

Bottom line you're pretty much the same person as you are right now if you have money or you don't. (I should point out here that 'won' money versus 'earnt' money affects people very differently. For example, the people who win money on the Lotto know from day one that they didn't earn it, they won it. The mental and emotional dynamics are totally different and are usually far more destructive to people who win money.)

There is a *however*, however. Just because *you* stay pretty much the same to the people around you once you get money, people may change toward *you*. If you are fortunate to receive a windfall of cash during your entrepreneur journey, be cautious with how you receive and distribute it. It will be impossible for friends, family and people in your social circle not to be aware of your change in fortune as you increase the material items that were always part of your vision for your life. But try to be considerate of how you evolve into this new identity for *them*. How they feel about your newfound wealth, how they fit into your life.

Remember, people only see the success, they never see and will never understand the sacrifices you made in order to achieve your vision. You'll figure this out on your own, but this is a heads up that you need to keep an eye on yourself, even with your generosity, which can backfire. Keep it real and don't believe your own hype!

The reality of getting more money is no different than when you get a raise at work. For a month or two its great and you enjoy the extra cash. But within about six months, you don't even notice it and your lifestyle has adjusted so that it's been absorbed into how you live day to day. A 2010 Study of over 450,000 people by Princeton University's Woodrow Wilson School showed that the correlation between a person's perceived happiness and wealth ends at earnings of $75,000 a year. So, in broad terms, once you hit that earning level, earning any more, doesn't make you any happier for any material *length* of time. Money loses its 'hit' value.

Now, I'm not saying having a lot of money isn't a great thing. It is! It allows you to buy more time for yourself and your family and buy the things you always wanted. Money doesn't change you, but it can change the way you live.

Don't get me wrong; it's fantastic to own luxury cars, houses and the best of everything. But, *ownership is a mirage.* It's not real, nor tangible for any lasting sense of self-fulfillment thru achievement. Attaining material ownership of things, in itself, will never be a successful end game vision outcome. What I am saying is that *just* having money as a measure of success is a mirage. Be warned! Its effect is *fleeting* and for anyone who has been building a business *just* for the money, it's usually a dangerous anticlimax. You'll never get 'there' if it's just about the money.

Here's a quick example of what I mean. I remember sharing a taxi with a guy who was worth over $300 million at the time. I remember it because the guy was visually stressed about an investment that had performed poorly for him and he had taken a relatively small financial hit. He was red in the face, sweating, not happy. Far from happy in fact. *I never understood that.* The guy is worth $300m. I never wanted to be that guy. I found the sole pursuit of money for success ugly, never ending and unfulfilling. You create no value by just pursuing cash. If this is for you, go be a banker, you don't have the creativity to be a successful entrepreneur.

SHOUTOUT: The only currency of any value is how we feel.

Now, I know what you're thinking, it's easy to say all this once you've got the new, big house, new car and expensive stuff right! Well, yes, it is easy to say. But you're reading this book to get a head start. To fast track. It's important to understand at this stage, that you will achieve your vision if you want it. *Really* want it. That you will get what you want. Respect the Journey and all the elements of it. The 'there' part is as good as you visualize it to be, so visualize your *life*, not just your possessions.

The single most important piece of advice I can offer would be this; *be careful what you wish for*, because you just might get it. When you do, it had better have been worth it, because you will have likely paid a high entrance fee, one way or another, to get it.

Ernest Hemmingway said; 'Nobility does not come from feeling superiority above your fellow man, true nobility comes from feeling superiority from your former self'.

Your journey is not about how you're doing against the *other* guy. It's about how you're doing against the inner guy. It's about how you rank against yourself compared to last year. How you are improving yourself. How you rank your own progress, your own performance, and your personal achievement. You're on the journey of 'you' and this is a big moment in your story. You saw it all the way through from vision to reality. This is a big part of the euphoria. It's the sense of self-progress that is a slow burning, good vibe feeling. This is not fleeting.

As time goes on and you settle into your 'there' life and you start to reflect how you got there, you connect the dots of the journey. It all starts making sense. The crazy situations, the crazy work hours, the failures, the successes, all the details and it dawns on you that it's actually the *journey itself*, and the people you meet on the journey, the Stories, that's the real fun of it all.

Once you're there, you will enjoy accolades from friends, family, your colleagues, investors and people you met along the way, but the real sense of achievement comes from inside you. From a deep connection you have with yourself that this was the *right thing* to be doing with your life, that you would not be defeated and that you saw this journey through. The ultimate accolade is from yourself, for yourself. It is the sense of progress against your own evaluation, your own scorecard. It's a recognition of how far you have come and the self-serving gratification and understanding that you are a more evolved version of yourself than when you started.

SHOUTOUT: The ultimate accolade is from yourself, for yourself.

We all want success. In many and any forms, but what is success when you boil it right down? *It's how we feel.* Do we *feel* successful? I've often said that the only currency of any value is *how I feel*. I've been a happy poor man and I've been an unhappy wealthy man. "Success" is actually an umbrella word. It's a headline. I think the feeling of true and sustainable success comes from meeting our universal human needs; significance, belonging, fulfillment, purpose and most of all, *progress* towards an evolved version of yourself as you have visualized it. Let's refrain from the pursuit of happiness. Let's pursue *progress*. Which leads to fulfillment, which I believe, is what leads to happiness and eventual self-actualization as Maslow describes in his Hierarchy of Needs. As I said in the beginning, *Purpose* is the engine of *Progress*. Progress is the fuel of *fulfillment*. Fulfillment is the road to *happiness*.

It's about being the best version of yourself that you can imagine and achieve. Continuous self-progress is the long burn reward of success.

> **ENTREPRENEURSHIP IS LIVING A FEW YEARS OF YOUR LIFE LIKE MOST PEOPLE WON'T, SO THAT YOU CAN SPEND THE REST OF YOUR LIFE LIKE MOST PEOPLE CAN'T.**

SHOUTOUT: Share when you're 'there'.

Another interesting point I have observed during my journey is that the entrepreneur fire *doesn't go out*. It never goes out, regardless of your success level. Being an entrepreneur is akin to an incurable disease. Like many creative people, you can't decide one day *not* to write music, or paint, or dance. Being an entrepreneur is *not optional.*

There is no 'off' switch, even when you want to switch it off. It doesn't work like that. The fire *never* goes out. The entrepreneur observation process can't be blinded. The curious, questioning, disrupting, evaluating process can't be overruled by accepting the world around us 'as is'. It's not even a choice. It's a lifestyle and a perspective on your lifestyle that defines your personality as an entrepreneur.

SHOUTOUT: The entrepreneur fire never goes out.

Generally speaking, people like a success story, especially if it's an underdog success story, as many entrepreneur journeys are. So, once you find yourself 'there', *share it*. I don't mean simply sharing the wealth with philanthropy and charitable contributions, I mean share your story, share your time and your knowledge. It will inspire other people to get started on their journey too. It gives them validation that it's possible, that success is not some elusive experience only for the few. It's for *everyone* who chooses the path. We can all experience a successful journey of self-development in whatever form is right for us. Sharing your journey once you're 'there' provides a validation to those still *on* the journey, or those who are just thinking about the Journey, that it really is attainable. Part of my reasoning to write this book is to share my journey so far, to hopefully fast track *your* journey, through my lessons and experiences. Doing so makes me *feel* successful and that's the *point*. The continuous pursuit of self-progress; that we feel contentment, significance, that we provide a contribution and by doing so, find our purpose. We evolve. We succeed. We are happy.

Success also makes you a *better* entrepreneur. Once you reach your 'there' point, and there may be several over the course of your life, you can enjoy the sharing process more than you can at the early stages of your entrepreneur journey. You also now have something that you didn't have when you are in the early stages of your journey, *credibility*. *You have done it.* The credibility is recognition, not only to yourself, but also to the world. Once you have this, your confidence to achieve your vision improves your approach to getting to the next 'there', or next big idea, it transcends into a calmer, more experienced process of Imagine, Believe, and

Achieve. Like anything, the more times you do it, the better you get at it.

One of my big 'there' moments. Signing the papers to sell my largest business to date aged forty-six.

That's it!

That's all I can give you at this stage of my journey. I hope the pages of this book made sense, had impact on you, resonated with you and most importantly, helped shape what you *already* knew. That you have all you need to get on with the journey right now. It's time to make your own choices and live your own journey. I hope the words empower you to harness your energy in a constructive way to achieve your vision of 'there'.

You have as good a chance as anyone else. Don't be selfish. Share it!
Go for it.

Ultimately, our choices, focus and sacrifices determine our outcome. You haven't come this far, just to come *this* far have you? However tough it's been, however tough it's going to get, remember, it's always better to go slowly, than to quit. Whatever your journey to this point has been remember this; you haven't got the power to change the past, so learn from it and let it go. It's not about where you are today, it's about where you *want* to be. You have the choice to start building your future. Decide *now*. You have control over your choices, your mindset and your effort.

Think big. You are the magic.

It's your move. It's your Journey…

What are you waiting for?

Aint Nothin' To It, But To Do It.

Chapter 14
Sources and Further Reading

Though much of this book is based on my personal experiences, I conducted additional research so that my information would be as up to date and accurate as possible. The sources I used are copied below, along with some additional resources that interested readers might find valuable.

Sources

www.sba.gov BizBuySell.com www.mbda.gov

US Bureau of Labor Statistics

CrunchBase; Various sources (Orrick, Startup Europe and European Commission); MTB; ID 885893 'UK House of Commons Library Briefing Paper 06152 Dec 2018

https://www.apa.org/topics/divorce/Source:https://eu.usatoday.com/story/money/ economy/2018/02/02/broken-hearts-rundown-divorce-capital-every-state/1078283001/

https://quickbooks.intuit.com/r/how-to-start-a-business/ http://www.hopesandfears.com/hopes/city/city_index/214133-city-index-marriage-lengths

https://www.bls.gov/bdm/entrepreneurship/bdm_chart3.htm

http://cosmetics.specialchem.com/news/industry-news/global-toothpaste-market- to-reach-usd14-billion-by-2020-global-industry-analysts

https://www.fool.com/careers/2017/05/03/what-percentage-of-businesses-fail-in- their-first.aspx

https://papers.ssrn.com/sol3/papers.cfm?abstract_id=933932

Suggested Resources

http://www.vincentwee.com/8-facts-startups-will-blow-mind/

https://hbr.org/2012/09/how-bad-leadership-spurs-entrepreneurship?aw id=8759529350471588839-3271

https://www.themuse.com/advice/14-things-no-one-tells-you-about-starting- a-business

https://www.entrepreneur.com/article/308447\\ *http://fortune.com/25/09/2014/why-startups-fail-according-to-their-founders/*
https://www.entrepreneur.com/article/285079

https://centreforentrepreneurs.org/cfe-releases/2016-breaks-business-formation- records/

https://www.fundera.com/blog/what-percentage-of-small-businesses-fail

https://www.inc.com/thomas-koulopoulos/5-of-the-most-surprising-statistics- about-start-ups.html

https://blogs.wsj.com/experts/2015/01/29/the-surprising-relatively-old-age-of- entrepreneurs/

https://smallbiztrends.com/11/2016/startup-statistics-small-business.html https://quickbooks.intuit.com/r/how-to-start-a-business/ https://quickbooks.intuit.com/r/trends-stats/know-small-businesses-start-10000-less/ https://www.inc.com/associated-press/small-business-sales-commodities-2017.html http://seriousstartups.com/2014/01/28/18-surprising-facts-entrepreneurship/ https://www.llewellyn.com/encyclopedia/article/244 https://study.com/academy/lesson/reticular-activating-system-definition-function.html https://townsquared.com/ts/resources/small-business-united-states-numbers/ https://www.sba.gov/sites/default/files/FAQ_Sept_2012.pdf https://www.sba.gov/content/small-business-gdp-update-2002-2010 https://www.bls.gov/bdm/us_age_naics_00_table7.txt

https://about.americanexpress.com/sites/americanexpress.newshq.businesswire.com/ files/doc_library/file/2017_SWOB_Report_-FINAL.pdf

https://www.inc.com/bill-carmody/why-96-of-businesses-fail-within-10-years.html

www.ingramcontent.com/pod-product-compliance
Lightning Source LLC
Chambersburg PA
CBHW070637220526
45466CB00001B/201